Ahsan Academy of Research
(Springs, South Africa)

The Codification of Islamic Law

Mawlānā Muhammad Abdul Aleem Siddiqui al-Qadri

Tawasul International
Centre for Publishing, Research and Dialogue

First Published 2024

ISBN: 9791281473300

Ahsan Academy of Research
(Springs, South Africa)
ahsan@worldonline.co.za

SHELVCRAFT™
Shelving | Racking | Display | Shop Fitting Ph:
012 666 8933
Email: sales@shelvcraft.com
Website: www.shelvcraft.com

Published by
Tawasul International
Centre for Publishing, Research and Dialogue, Rome, Italy

CONTENTS

Foreword

His Eminence Mawlānā Abdul Aleem Siddiqui Al-Qādri (may Allah bless him) was one of the most gifted intellectuals of his time. His rational approach to present day problems displayed his depth of knowledge, clarity of thought, deep acumen, and breadth of vision. The exquisitely charming and lucid narration of the historical evidence by the learned author conclusively establishes the veracity and authenticity of the codified Islamic law as projected in the four schools of thought.

The reader would observe that His Eminence (may Allah bless him) had addressed the issue of the codification of Islamic law in the mid- nineteenth century as part of the lecture programme during his missionary sojourn to the island of Trinidad in West Indies, South America.

Mawlānā Siddiqui's spiritual and intellectual prowess had perceived the magnitude of the problem and his discerning mind had seen the seed of discord that would result in the division of the Muslim community and thus weaken the ummah. At this point in time, we are witnessing deep cracks in the body politic of Islam, once considered impregnable.

The division in supposedly the largest religious majority in the world despite the authenticity and purity of the Divine Scripture and the legacy of the ahādith has been primarily due to the acute lethargy of the Muslim community to study and follow the path as ordained in the Qur'ān and sunnah. The apathy towards serious consideration of the purpose of creation of mankind as stated in the Qur'ān is disturbing to say the least. Our muddled orientation fails to grasp the reality of life and the purpose defined in the Qur'ān by Allah. Thus, the Muslim ummah has fallen into the abyss of ignorance of the Divine Guidance.

Materialism in common parlance has so captivated the attention of the individual member of the present-day society that he can give but scant attention to the Islamic norms and values in real life. His thought format has its roots in the secular system of education provided in the formal schools of today, adding to his vulnerability on issues which look innocuous superficially but cause confusion.

Moreover, if such issues are not provided with logical explanation it can result result in weakened belief. Contorted perceptions today find easier dissemination through print and electronic media in the global village and have caused tremendous damage to the unity of the Muslim ummah. More than ever before, the correct presentation of Islam, strictly based on Qur'ān and sunnah, needs to be projected through the media following in the footsteps of ʿulamā such as Mawlānā Abdul Aleem Siddiqui (may Allah bless him).

"Allah will exalt those who believe among you, and those who have knowledge, to high ranks" (58:11)

Mustafa F. Ansari
Honorary Secretary General
World Federation of Islamic Missions, Islamic Centre,
Block-B, North Nazimabad, Karachi.

Chapter 1

Some Basic Observations

In my class lectures and public speeches, I have already explained the obvious truth that only the inventor and manufacturer of a machine knows best how to use it and he alone can properly teach its use to others. I have also explained that every maker holds his creation dear and does not like it to be spoiled in any way, and that, consequently, he teaches its method of use himself.

I have also explained and proved by rational arguments that the. universe decidedly owes its existence to a Creator, for Whom every particle of the Creation is a witness. I also made it clear that, just as there are natural laws which govern the working of the universe (and they are called Allah's way in the Holy Qur'ān), similarly there are laws, ordained by Allah, relating to the individual and social life of human beings, and that it is Allah's Way to teach them to mankind, for which the divinely-appointed law of delivering Divine Guidance in the form of wahy (i.e. revelation) through the Prophets and Messengers endowed with special capacities by Allah to perform the task, has been coming into play since the creation of humanity.

I have further explained that humanity and its culture and civilization have grown gradually, that for a very long period the races and nations of the world remained divided and segregated from each other and that, during that period of immature humanity, separate Prophets, and Messengers of Allah continued to come to the separate human communities, so much so, that on certain occasions, more than one Prophet was working at the same time among different groups. However, when the time came for humanity to come together, when the age of the printing press and the wireless and the airplane dawned, when mankind arrived at the stage of its history where it could function as one body, when the human ingenuity was on the verge of developing those means whereby it could preserve the Divine Message for all time, Allah Almighty sent such a perfect guide, such a world Prophet and Messenger, who came with the title not of the Mercy for the Arabs but as the Mercy unto all the worlds, and Allah's Word was announced about him:

> "Verily, We have sent you not but as the Bringer of Glad Tidings and the Warner for the whole of humanity."

That great Prophet came transcending the limitations of country and clime. He came as the divine mercy personified. He came with the divine message of mercy, the revealed guidance, the divinely-appointed Law, the religion of mercy. His glorious name is MUHAMMAD, i.e., the Praised One, (pbuh). He was declared to be the Last Prophet. Prophethood found its consummation in his august person. Religion was perfected in all its aspects and one for all. The divine proclamation was made:

> "This day have I perfected your religion for you, completed My favour upon you, and have chosen for you Islam as your religion.[1]"

That great Prophet announced in unambiguous terms: "I am the last Prophet and there is no prophet after me"[2].

Humanity had received the perfect religion. Consequently, the door of divine revelation was closed and sealed, and Allah's last Prophet announced: "Nothing remains from the prophethood except true dreams". This was a statement meaning the divine revelation, which has been named in the Holy Qur'ān as wahy and which means positive and certain knowledge communicated by Allah, came to an end with the last Prophet.

In that -literal and certain revelation (wahy matlu) which was granted to that great Prophet, the divine promise of preserving it was affirmed. The Word of Allah proclaimed:

> "We have, without doubt, sent down the Message; We will assuredly guard it (from and corruption).[3]"

---

[1] *Al-Māʾidah 5:3.*
[2] Jamiʿ at-Tirmidhi, Hadith 2219, Book of Al-Fitan 33, Hadith 62.
[3] *Al-Hijr 15: 9.*

And, again:

"No falsehood can approach from before or behind it: It is
sent down by One, full of Wisdom, Worthy of all Praise.[4]"

For the preservation of the Message, Allah Almighty advised His
Holy Prophet (pbuh) the following words:

"Move not your tongue concerning (the Qur'ān) to make haste
therewith. It is for Us to collect it and to promulgate (or recite) it. So,
when We have promulgated (or recited) it, you follow its recital.[5]"

That was about the text of the Holy Qur'ān which is preserved
today not only in Book form but also in millions of human brains
(memory).

As for the preservation of the meanings of the Qur'ānic text, Allah
Almighty made it clear that:

Any more, it is for Us to explain it (and make it clear).[6]

Thus, it was not only the preservation of the text of the Holy
Qur'ān but also its meanings, which Allah Almighty took upon
Himself. Hence, the Holy Prophet (pbuh) said: "I have been given the
Qur'ān and the like of it along with it"[7].

This means that the Holy Prophet (pbuh) was not given only the
Qur'ānic text, but was also taught its meaning by Allah Almighty.

The Holy Prophet (pbuh), in his turn, transmitted the text as well
as the meaning to his Companions (Sahābah). Every student of the
hadith knows that the Companions would come to him, take lessons
from him in portions of the text along with their meanings and
explanations, and, in their turn, teach the same to others.

---

4 *Hā Mim Al-Sajdah 41: 42.*
5 *Al-Qiyāmah 75: 16-18.*
6 *Al-Qiyāmah 75: 19.*
7 Sunan Abi Dawud 4604, Book of Adherence To The Sunnah 42, Hadith 9.

Thus, on the other hand, the Holy Prophet (pbuh) transmitted the actual meanings and true explanation of the Holy Qur'ān to his Companions through them to the later generations, those who might wish to change the meanings and the explanations. He said:

"Whosoever explains the Holy Qur'ān according to his personal opinion, let him make his abode in Hell."[8]

He further warned those might attribute false explanations or forged hadith to his name, saying:

"Whosoever intentionally attributes a false thing to me, let him make his abode in Hell."[9]

Then, after he had taken all the steps for preserving the teachings of Islam, the Holy Prophet (pbuh) informed the world that:

"One party of my followers will always remain above others with clear truth. Whosoever opposes them will not be able to harm them (i.e. overpower them in argument), until the Last Day."[10]

In the light of the preliminaries outlined, I am sure you have understood fully that the Islam which comprehends that Islamic law (shari`ah), is based, from the beginning to the end, on wahy which will remain in its original purity (Inshā-Allah) to the Last Day. Every word of the Holy Qur'ān is from Allah, and for the explanation of every word the personal guidance (or sunnah) of the Holy Prophet (pbuh) is present.

Thus, when Sayyidah A'isha, the truthful, (Allah be pleased with her!) was asked about the morals and manners of the Holy Prophet (pbuh), she replied: "His morals are the Qur'ān"[11], which means that

---

[8] Jami` at-Tirmidhi 2950, Book of Tasir 47, Hadith 1.
[9] Sahih al-Bukhari 109, Book of Knowledge 3, Hadith 51.
[10] Sahih Muslim 1923, Book of Government 33, Hadith 249.
[11] Al-Adab Al-Mufrad, Book of Excellence in Character 14, Hadith 308.

the Holy Prophet (pbuh)'s actions and sayings were the practical commentary of the Holy Qur'ān. In other words, the Holy Prophet (pbuh) was the embodiment of action based upon the Holy Qur'ān. (May his memory be ever green!).

It is because of this that Allah ordered us in the Holy Qur'ān:

> "So, take what the Apostle assigns to you and deny yourselves that which he withholds from you.[12]"

And, again:

> "Verily, in the Messenger of Allah there is for you the best model.[13]"

We are further told with great emphasis that every action and saying of the Holy Prophet (pbuh) is thoroughly based on revelation from Allah. Thus, the Holy Qur'ān says:

> "Nor does he say (anything) of (his own) desire. It is no less than revelation sent down to him.[14]"

Still more emphatic is the following Qur'ānic verse:

> "Verily, those who give their pledge to you (0 Prophet!) do nothing less than give their pledge to Allah: The Hand of Allah is over their hands.[15]"

Further, the Holy Qur'ān describes the act of the Holy Prophet (pbuh) as the act of Allah, It says, while referring to the Holy Prophet (pbuh)'s act of throwing dust towards the enemy during the battle of Badr:

---

[12] *Al-Hashr 59: 7.*
[13] *Al-Ahzāb 33: 21.*
[14] *Al-Najm 53: 3-4.*
[15] *Al-Fath 48: 10.*

"When you threw (a handful of dust), it was not your act, but Allah's.[16]"

Thus, at another place, the Holy Qur'ān says:

"He who obeys the Apostle, obeys Allah.[17]"

Hence, the basis of the Islamic religion and law is first the divinely revealed Guidance existing in the form of the Holy Qur'ān and second the sunnah (personal guidance) of the Holy Prophet (pbuh) which is nothing else than a practical and magnified reflection of the Holy Qur'ān.

It was this fundamental importance of the Holy Prophet (pbuh)'s sunnah which compelled the early Muslims to observe extreme caution in receiving and transmitting the Prophetic traditions (ahādith). The Companions valued every saying of the Holy Prophet (pbuh) as the greatest treasure, strived their utmost to preserve it, and understood every teaching of the Holy Qur'ān in the light of those ahādith.

In the preliminary remarks, I have made it plain that the Prophet of Islam was the last Prophet, after whom no one is to receive prophethood, and that the law which humanity has received through him is the perfect law, after which no further law is needed and which stands as the code of guidance for humanity till the Last Day. In fat, the Holy Qur'ān claims, and history supports this claim, that whatever the new forms which human problems might take and however complex may be the issues confronting humanity, the Qur'ānic guidance is always competent to meet the new situation. Allah himself describes the Holy Qur'ān as:

"The Book which explains all things.[18]"

This comprehensive and fundamental guidance, received in the light of the Holy Prophet (pbuh)'s sunnah, and acted upon, is always

---

[16] *Al-Anfāl 8: 17.*
[17] *Al-Nisā 4: 80.*
[18] *Al-Nahl 16: 89.*

sufficient and always unfailing.

There may, however be certain points of detail which might come into existence in a certain situation, and the guidance on that point might be implicit and not explicit in the Qur'ān and the sunnah. In such a situation, there arises the need for qiyās (analogy) which consists in discovering the implied guidance of the Qur'ān and the sunnah on the point concerned. The work of qiyās is to be performed by the experts of Islamic learning and its Qur'ānic sanction is found in the verses which I shall presently quote. The Holy Qur'ān says:

Do they not ponder over (the teachings of) the Qur'ān.[19]

About those who carry out this work of pondering, the Holy Qur'ān says:

"He granted wisdom to whom He pleased; and he to whom wisdom is granted received indeed a benefit overflowing; but none will grasp the Message save men of understanding.[20]"

We are again told in a hadith:

"To whomsoever Allah wills good, He grants him the understanding of religion."[21]

The Holy Qur'ān further emphasizes this tafaqquh, this "understanding of religion" by saying:

"If a group from every party remained; behind, they could devote themselves to studies religion, and admonish the people when they return to them...[22]"

At another place, the Holy Qur'ān says:

---

[19] *Al-Nisā 4: 80.*
[20] *Al-Baqarah 2: 269.*
[21] Sahih al-Bukhari 71, Book of Knowledge 3, Hadith 13.
[22] *Al-Tawbah: 9: 122.*

And those who are firmly grounded in knowledge say: "We believe in The Book; the whole of it is from our Lord and none will grasp the Message except men of understanding."[23]

Speaking about these men of understanding (fuqahā), the Holy Qur'ān further observes:

"Do those who know and those who do not know stand on the same footing.[24]"

Then the Holy Qur'ān makes it clear as to who, even among the educated, is entitled to be considered a true scholar of religion. It is emphatic in pointing out that the understanding of religion, the wisdom, the firm grounding in knowledge, does not consist merely in reading certain books. Nay, it rather says:

"Verily, they alone are (true) scholars (of religion) who fear Allah.[25]"

Thus, the basic qualification is fear of Allah (taqwā). Only those who, side by side with their pursuit of formal education, cultivate their spirituality, whose hearts become the seat of the fear of Allah, who, in every action and in every saying, remember their accountability before Allah, who, in short, remain absorbed in the remembrance of Allah (dhikr) - they alone are considered by the Holy Qur'ān as men of understanding. This is what we are told in a verse which reads:

"Verily, in the creation of the heavens and the earth, and in the alternation of the night and day, there are signs for men of understanding- those who remember Allah standing, sitting and reclining on their sides and who ponder on the creation of the heavens and the earth..."

---

[23] *Āl 'Imrān* 3: 7.
[24] *Al-Zumar* 39: 9.
[25] *Fātir* 35: 28.

Their absorption in the remembrance of Allah ultimately reveals to them the realities behind things, until they cry out:

"O our Lord! You have not created all this in vain! Glory be to You! Preserve us from the doom of fire.[26]"

Therefore, understanding of religion and the grasp of the problems of Islamic law form part of that real opening up of the heart referred to just now. The next step is the realisation of the higher verities, like the Attributes of Allah, etc.

This is the group who have been called the Ahl- al-Dhikr "(i.e., persons who truly grasp the Message) in the Holy Qur'ān, which, as we have seen before, describes itself as Al-Dhikr (see Al-Hijr 15:9). It is these Ahl-al-Dhikr, these persons who combine spiritual illumination with the religious knowledge of a very high level, whom the Holy Qur'ān regards above the rest. In fact, it invites t e general Muslims to take them as their teachers and to accept their legal deductions, for it clearly lays down this principle:

"Enquire from the Ahl-al-Dhikr if you do not know.[27]"

The Holy Qur'ān is clear and plain. We have not been permitted to interpret its teachings in the light of our own little education and meagre understanding. For, by interpreting them in the light of our pre-conceived opinions and prejudices, we earn nothing but Hell, as the Holy Prophet (pbuh) made it clear in the hadith quoted before.

Again, because of the lack of comprehensive vision, we shall at best have a partial view of the problem. That must land us in wrong conclusions. Thus, the animal self (nafs-al-ammārah) within the sphere of physical pleasures will leads us to all sorts of sins. It is only when we subject ourselves to impartial guidance that we can hope to escape the deceptions of our prejudices.

Those who introduce their personal opinions and desires into the interpretations of religious matters may well remember the

---

[26] *Āl ʿImrān 3: 191.*
[27] *Al-Nahl 16: 43.*

powerful and fundamental condemnation by the Holy Qur'ān in the fallowing words:

Do you see such b one who takes for his Allah his own passion (or impulse)? Could you be the disposer of affairs for him? or, do you think that most of them listen or understand? They are only like cattle; Nay, they are worse astray in the right way.[28]

He who glories in personal judgment without possessing the qualifications laid down by the Qur'ān, will find, on honest self-examination, that he is deceiving both himself and others. The primary force in all such cases is the desire to follow one's passions rather than to subject oneself to the discipline of the Qur'ān and the sunnah.

It is to save us from such pitfalls that the Holy Qur'ān has ordered us to seek guidance form the Ahl adh-Dhikr, from those true experts of Islamic learning, who because of their spiritual purity, are capable of seeing things impartially, whose lives are the embodiment of the fear of Allah, who, when they interpreted the Holy Qur'ān and the hadith, do not rely on their individual opinions, but exert fully to know and understand the conclusions which other experts have arrived at. They do not suffer from self-worship and egotism, but proceed in their search of the solution with all humility and in conformity with the view of most of the leaders of Islamic knowledge (fuqahā). Such a consensus of opinion when arrived at the solution of some new legal detail is known as the ijmā`.

Thus, we find there are four bases or sources of the codified Islamic Law, namely:

1. The Book of Allah (Qur'ān).
2. The sunnah of the Prophet of Allah.
3. Understanding and analogy (qiyās).
4. Consensus of expert opinion (ijmā`).

Let us now cast a glance at history and see how the Islamic law assumed the codified form.

---

[28] *Al-Furqān* 25: 43-44.

Chapter 2

Arrangement and Compilation of the Holy Qur'ān

You might have heard that the Holy Qur'ān was not delivered to the Holy Prophet (pbuh) just once as a complete book, but was revealed to him bit by bit and piece by piece, through the Archangel Jibrail (peace be with him).

The Holy Prophet (pbuh) had completed forty years of his age and was engaged in a special form of communion with Allah in the solitude of the Cave of Hira, when the angel first appeared before him and delivered before him the first revelation which reads:

> "Read! in the name of thy Lord and Cherisher, who created - created man, out of a (mere) clot of congealed blood: Read! And your Lord is Most Bountiful - Who taught (the use of) the Pen - taught man that which he knew not.[1]"

After an interval, came the second revelation:

> "O you wrapped up (in your mantle)! Arise and deliver your warning! And your Lord do you magnify! And your garments keep free from stain! And all abomination shuns! Nor expect in giving any increase (for yourself)![2]"

Thereafter commenced the general preaching and the invitation went forth to accept the divine message. The members of the powerful tribe of the Quraish were invited to assemble and to hear the Holy Prophet (pbuh)'s first sermon on the Mount. The message of the Unity of Allah (tawhid) was proclaimed aloud, and polytheism and infidelity (shirk) were condemned in the most unambiguous terms.

In the meantime, revelations continued to come. The Holy Prophet

---

[1] *Al-'Alaq 96: 1-5.*
[2] *Al-Muddaththir 74: 1-6.*

(pbuh) would remember them himself and would teach them to his Companions, like Khadijah, Abu Bakr, and Ali (May Allah be pleased with them), so that they could remember them by heart.

A race illiterate as the Arabs, there were very few in Makkah who could read or write. There was no paper, and the pen and the inkpot were scarce. It was, indeed, a most difficult task to get the revelations written down as they came. But the arrangement was made. A few of those who knew the art of writing embraced Islam. The verses of the Holy Qur'ān were inscribed on palm-leaves and leather sheets. Some of the Companions were specially charged with the duty of learning the portions of the Qur'ān as they were revealed. Persons were specially selected from among the Companions who would take lessons from the Holy Prophet (pbuh) each lesson consisting of ten verses of the Holy Qur'ān. They would learn those verses by heart and learn their meanings and interpretations as taught by the Holy Prophet (pbuh) and teach the same to others.

Then came the time of the migration to Madinah (hijrah). The Muslim group had been growing gradually. At Madinah it was knit into a functioning community. Among other things, the Holy Prophet (pbuh) made the arrangements whereby a larger number of Companions could learn to read and write. The work of writing down the revelations of the Qur'ān continued with the fullest devotion. Its compilation in the form of a scripture was attended to. Zaid bin Thābit, who was a freed slave, was one of those Companions who were entrusted with the task of writing down the Qur'ān. The revelations continued to come and they were not only preserved in writing, but the Holy Prophet (pbuh) under divine guidance, would fix up the chapters and would instruct the scribes to insert a certain revelation at a certain place in a certain chapter.

Gradually, the delivery of the Word of Allah reached completion and, at the Farewell Pilgrimage, in the plain of Arafat, came the revelation:

"This day I have perfected your religion for you, completed my favor upon you and have chosen for you Islam as your religion.[3]"

Not only the arrangement of the verses and the fixing up of chapters was done by the Holy Prophet (pbuh) but he also fixed up the serial arrangement of the chapters, and all that he did under Divine instructions. To carry the work to its logical finish, Abu Bakr Siddiq, Islam's first Caliph, rendered the service of giving the separately written chapters the form of a consolidated compilation.

Different portions of the Qur'ān written by different people continued to remain, however, in their possession. The people of different places also continued to follow their local pronunciations of Qur'ānic verses.

Then came the period of the third Caliph, Uthman (May Allah be pleased with him). Islam was no more confined to Makkah and Madinah, but had crossed the boundaries of the Arabian Peninsula and had entered Egypt, Palestine, Syria, Iraq, and Iran. People were entering the fold of Islam in ever-growing numbers. The interest in Qur'ānic recitation was becoming universal. Large numbers of people had only portions of the Qur'ān in their possession. Misunderstandings could arise that only such and such a portion formed the whole Qur'ān, and that the other portions were not part of it. Hence, Caliph Uthman got several copies made of the manuscript compiled during Caliph Abu Bakr's caliphate (khilāfat) and sent those copies to the different centres of the Islamic empire. The copy which Caliph Uthman himself used for study and on which, it is said, the drops of his blood fell at the time of his martyrdom, remained preserved first at Madinah and was later transferred from there to the Imperial library of Istanbul by the Turkish sultans.

All the copies of the Holy Qur'ān which exist in the world today are true copies of the manuscript. Not only the Muslims, but also the opponents of Islam, find themselves compelled to admit that the Holy Qur'ān has maintained the original purity of its text, even to a letter.

As regards the vowels, it is customary in the Arabic language not to mention them in writing, because they are only symbolic and are

---

[3] *Al-Mā'idah 5: 3.*

not expressed in the letter- form. But when Islam spread among the non-Arab populations, those non-Arab Muslims had trouble in reading the Qur'ān. Hence under the orders of Hajjaj bin Yusuf, the vowel symbols were included in written copies according to the universal form in which thousands of Muslims had learnt the Qur'ānic text by heart, and which form had been transferred faithfully by the "preservers" (huffādh) from generation to generation. The seven styles of intonation (qirā'ah) which the Holy Prophet (pbuh) was himself taught by Allah, were taught to the people by qualified teachers. All those styles have been preserved down to the present day by hundreds of thousands of people, though there is one style which is more universal than the rest.

Thus, it is clear as daylight that the Qur'ān exists in the world today in its absolute original purity, and that, not only as a written text, but also in the memories of hundreds of thousands of Muslims which makes it impossible for anyone to effect the change even of a dot.

Chapter 3

Compilation of Prophetic Traditions
and Biographies of Reporters

It has been proved in the foregoing that the basis of understanding the Holy Qur'ān is the interpretation given by the Holy Prophet (pbuh) of Islam. The verses of the Qur'ān means that which the Holy Prophet (pbuh) understood and made us to understand, whether through action or through saying. Consequently, the Companions of the Holy Prophet (pbuh) were always extremely attentive to every word that he said and tried to remember it to the very letter. They were so cautious in the matter that if they ever apprehended that they had forgotten some actual word and had only remembered its synonym, they would always point it out while narrating a certain hadith. Thus, not only was the Holy Prophet (pbuh)'s life-account preserved for us, but also the solutions of the various problems of religion and law which the Holy Prophet (pbuh) gave.

When it was emphasized that the Holy Qur'ān should be written down, and arrangements were made accordingly. Some of the Companions thought of putting down the ahādith of the Holy Prophet (pbuh) also in writing. But, because Islam was still in its early stage, the Holy Prophet (pbuh) feared that if these were committed to writing side by side with the Qur'ān, people might get confused and might mix up both things. Hence, he forbade them in the beginning from doing so. However, when that danger had passed away and people were sufficiently trained to distinguish the Qur'ān from the hadith, he allowed them to write down his sayings. In fact, he himself got them written as, for instance, when he dictated the rules of Zakāt, etc., to Ali.

Among the Companions there were some who would pass their whole time, so to say, at the feet of the Holy Prophet (pbuh). Close to the Holy Prophet (pbuh)'s residential room and the mosque, there is a raised platform which is called Suffah. A party of students (Companions) used to occupy this platform permanently. Their work was to learn by heart whatever they heard from the Holy Prophet (pbuh). One of those people of Suffah was Abu Hurairah, who was endowed with a powerful memory and who remembered many the Holy Prophet (pbuh)'s traditions (ahādith) and reported them.

This I have related with a view to make you understand that, just as arrangements were made to preserve the Holy Qur'ān by means of writing and learning by heart, similarly did the Companions of the Holy Prophet (pbuh) exert themselves to preserve the Prophet's traditions. Their method consisted in learning them by heart and reporting them with all the care which the sacredness of the task and their devotion to the Holy Prophet (pbuh) and Islam demanded. One person reported to another, one generation reported to the other succeeding it. Thus, a continuous chain of reporters was built - a continuous chain through which passed the most valuable treasure of the Holy Prophet (pbuh)'s sayings and actions.

Now, the way in which this chain of reporters (isnād) was built up and the extremely critical method which gave luster to it, has made this chain one of the glories of Islamic history. The fact is, that the experts of historical science cannot produce another instance in world's history where those critical historical standards were observed which have gone to make the Hadith literature such an authentic record as it is.

If, today, I am asked to narrate a hadith to some scholar of that science, it will not be enough for me to recite its text. Rather, I will have to report my authority and I will have to prove that my chain of reporters is faultless and ends at the Holy Prophet (pbuh).

Indeed, those who were responsible for the compilation of hadith literature, observed a measure of care beyond which human endeavour could not go. In the case of each hadith that reached them, they examined its authenticity thoroughly. They tested the chain of reporters through which it was transmitted. They enquired whether a certain reporter had seen and met the other reporter from whom he claimed to have received the hadith. They saw whether the reporters were persons of good and reliable memory. They investigated piety and fear of Allah in the lives of the reporters. In short, they employed all conceivable standards for assessing the true worth of every hadith reported and accepted it only after they had been thoroughly satisfied.

This brings us to the fact that there were, and there are ahādith of different grades in accordance with their measure of authenticity. This grading was done on the basis of different factors. Variously, the considerations were (1) the moral condition of the reporters and the level of their piety; (2) the powers of memory which the reporters were found to possess; (3) intelligence and capacity to grasp religious truths; (4) consideration of the fact whether the report had come through one channel only or different channels, etc. When the details of the Islamic law were deduced, these factors governing the worth of different traditions were always kept in view.

In connection with the extreme caution which the compilers of hadith observed, I may mention here an incident of the life of Imām Muhammad bin Ismail Al- Bukhari, the leader of all compilers. The compendium of hadith which this great scholar has given to the world is the result of a most thorough sifting of hadith literature. His sense of respect which he had for the work he had in hand, and his piety and Allah-Awareness (taqwā), can be judged from the fact that when he was writing the Sahih-al-Bukhari, he made fresh ablution and offered two rakā'at of prayer before writing each individual hadith.

This great Imām once heard that at a long distance from his place there was some person who knew certain Sayings of the Holy Prophet (pbuh). The Imām undertook the arduous journey on foot to obtain from him the ahādith in question. When he at last arrived in the village where the man lived, he enquired his where-abouts. Someone pointed him out nearby. The man was busy calling his horse from a distance in order to attract him. Imām Bukhari went towards the man and the first thing he did was to cast a glance at the fodder can, which he found to be empty. At once the Imām retraced his steps. The man noticed it and was bewildered. He left the chase of the horse, ran towards the Imām, and requested him to explain the incident to him. The Imām replied: "I had heard that you relate traditions of the Holy Prophet (pbuh), and had therefore come after a long journey to meet you. But when I saw you calling the horse with an empty fodder can in your hand, I concluded that a person who can cheat a horse, is also capable of cheating men. I cannot accept any Hadith reported by such a person".

With such extreme care, the traditions were collected. This

extreme care was undertaken not only because of inherent necessity, but also because of the machinations some non-Muslim opponent of Islam. Some of these people have never left any stone unturned in scheming against Islam, although the Muslim governments always treated them most magnanimously and provided them asylum while the rest of the world was persecuting them. In those early days, they were hatching all sorts of plots to undermine Islam. They tried their hands at various schemes, but failed. At last, they planned to disguise as Muslims, to forge traditions in the name of the Holy Prophet (pbuh), and to propagate them amongst the Muslims, thereby aiming to contaminate the purity of Islamic teachings and to corrupt the Muslim religious life. Many such forged traditions were broadcast among the Muslims. The scholars of Islam, who had been forewarned by the Holy Prophet (pbuh) about the appearance of such a menace, were soon on their guard. They built up a whole science of historical criticism, and compiled extensive works on the biographies of reporters, whereby a genuine tradition could be correctly distinguished from a forged one.

I may here remark in passing that certain persons of our own times have tried to tamper with the hadith literature to suit their own ends, though their method has been different. They could not forge new traditions, having appeared so late in Islamic History. They tried to fall back upon the forged or weak traditions handed down from the past. But that, too, could not work in view of the smashing criticism from the side of the experts of the science of Tradition. So, one of them, namely, Mirza Ghulam Ahmad of Qadiani when he found that his claims could not be comfortably lodged in genuine traditions, fell back upon the arbitrary assertion that he was the divinely appointed judge and could, therefore, accept any tradition he liked and reject any other he did not like, the principles of logical and historical criticism notwithstanding.

In connection with our discussion of hadith and sunnah, there is an important point which may well be kept in mind.

We have already seen that the Holy Qur'ān was revealed bit by bit. The commandments were delivered gradually to progressively reclaim and reform a people who were diseased, deformed, and corrupt beyond limit. Had they been subjected to the complete discipline of Islam from the very first day, they would have in all probability found it psychologically too heavy to carry and to follow. Take, for instance, the case of alcoholic drinks. As all students of Arab history know, side by side with idolatry and polytheism and various spiritual and moral evils, the liquor habit was embedded so deeply in the lives of the Arab that any other race of the world could hardly claim a higher degree of addiction. Had the law of prohibition been imposed on them forthwith, their psychological condition and diseased nervous state would have compelled them to sacrifice imān and Islam to alcohol. They would have preferred the latter to the former. But infidelity and polytheism are root-sins which entitle man to nothing less than eternal fire, while other sins, whether major or minor, stand below in degree. If the root of a tree is healthy and safe, whatever the calamities which might afflict other parts, there is always the hope that the tree can survive. But once the root is diseased or is removed, the whole tree is bound to perish once for all. Hence, in the case of wine, the polite commandment was revealed first. It laid down:

Approach not prayers while intoxicated.[1]

Later on, came the second revelation in the same connection and contained the exhortation that:

"In them (that is, wine and gambling) is great sin, and some profit, for men; but the sin is greater than the profit."[2]

When thus, people had been ultimately taught to hate wine, the final commandment came:

"O you who believe! Intoxicants and gambling, (dedication of) stones and (divination by) arrows, are abomination - of Satan's handiwork: Eschew such (abomination), that you may

---

[1] *Al-Nisā* 4: 43.
[2] *Al-Baqarah* 2: 219.

prosper."[3]

The result of adopting the gradual procedure was that when total prohibition was announced, people immediately broke into pieces the vessels of wine, and the liquor from the broken jars was flowing in the streets of Madinah.

Here you can understand the problem of the abrogation of verses also easily, which might be explained to you fully on some later occasion. In this connection we might keep in mind the fact that whatever commandments were revealed on any occasion they were invariably based on wisdom. However, when a certain commandment referred to a passing situation, it was replaced by another at a later stage. Such commandments did not mean calling the same thing "white" on one occasion and "black" on another. They rather represented the progressive revelation of guidance in connection with the gradual reformation of the first Islamic community.

We have seen, in the case of wine, that, in the early days of Islam those who were addicted to it continued to use it, only abstaining from it during prayer times, until the commandment relating to total prohibition was revealed. Now, it is quite conceivable that those Muslims who lived at a long distance from Madinah, might have continued to act according to the first injunction even some time after the revelation of the final commandment. The means of communication were very meagre in those days, especially in a backward country like Arabia. The issue of prohibition was, however, a very vital one. Hence the Islamic community at Madinah made the utmost effort for making Allah's final commandment known to everyone and within a short time it reached every ear.

But, think now, in the light of this, about the information reaching the people concerning the Holy Prophet (pbuh)'s sayings and actions. Suppose the Holy Prophet (pbuh) acted in some matter in a certain way in the light of certain special considerations, and suppose some Companions from outside Madinah were present with him on that occasion, and they carried with them to their homes the

---

[3] *Al-Māʾidah 5: 90.*

memory of that incident and preserved it in their minds for guidance.

However, after some days the Holy Prophet (pbuh) acted in some similar matter differently, under Divine guidance. And this did not reach those who had observed his previous action.

Now, suppose the two different actions related to some minor affair which was not of such a serious importance as the issue 'of liquor prohibition referred to and was not broadcast in the same manner. Therefore, those who knew only the Holy Prophet (pbuh)'s previous action continued to be guided by it. Certainly, their motive was to follow the Holy Prophet (pbuh)'s way and hence their action was right. But those who had the opportunity of observing the Holy Prophet (pbuh)'s later action and made it their guiding principle, were right, the more so.

Apparently, the stands of the two parties became different in that matter. But both were sincere in their motives. And it is this to which the Holy Prophet (pbuh) referred when he said:

"The differences of my people are (based on) mercy."[4]

Those differences were not grounded in selfishness, egotism, and stubbornness, nor were they created by the claims of false prophets and so-called reformers, as is the case now-a-days, but they always rose up in the purest motives and in the devotion to the Holy Prophet (pbuh).

I may explain to you the nature of those early differences further. Once the Holy Prophet (pbuh) ordered a party of his Companions to go to a certain place, offer their `Asr prayers there, perform certain work, and return. The party started for the place forthwith. But they were still on the way when they found that the time for `Asr was about to expire. The party split into two groups on the interpretation of the Holy Prophet (pbuh)'s command. One group said that when the Holy Prophet (pbuh) gave them that command, what he meant was that the party should proceed with all possible haste and not

---

[4] Al-Bayhaqī on the authority of Abd Allāh ibn ʿAbbās, considered by many Hadith scholars as a weak tradition.

that they should forego offering the Asr prayer within time. The other group insisted that the Holy Prophet (pbuh) was himself the law-giver and his command to offer the `Asr prayer after reaching the place was meant to be carried out as it stood. Both the groups offered the prayer according to their decisions. When the party returned, they submitted their difference of opinion to the Holy Prophet (pbuh). He smiled and said that both were right because the motive of both was to obey him. The difference consisted only in interpretation. One group emphasized the letter, while the other emphasized the spirit.

Thus, we know that differences of opinion arose even among the Companions. But those differences related only to honest understanding of problems and had nothing to do with personal jealousies, quarrels, and rivalries.

In a word, differences of opinion among the Companions came into existence on the basis of either of the two causes:

1. when a certain tradition reached one group and did not reach another.
2. differences of understanding and interpretation.

Chapter 4

Preservers of Hadith and Scholars of Law
among the Companions

The students of Islamic history know that all the Companions of the Holy Prophet (pbuh) did not enjoy the same status in respect of guiding the people in matters of religion and law. Those who had passed most of their time from the beginning of the prophetic period in the company of the Holy Prophet (pbuh), those whom the Holy Prophet (pbuh) himself would consult in Islamic matters, those whose great qualities were commended by no less a person than the Holy Prophet (pbuh) (pbuh) were persons head and shoulders above the rest. The Holy Prophet (pbuh) called Abu Bakr (may Allah be pleased with him) as the greatest person outside the category of prophets. He said about Umar (may Allah be pleased with him): "If there had been a prophet after me, Umar would have been that Prophet." He described Uthman (may Allah be pleased with him) as the most perfect in piety. He observed about Ali (may Allah be pleased with him): "I am the city of knowledge, and Ali is its gate." Similarly distinguished were: A'isha (may Allah be pleased with her), the beloved wife of the Holy Prophet (pbuh), Abdullah bin Umar (may Allah be pleased with him), Abdullah bin Mas`ud; (R.A.), Abdullah bin Abbas (may Allah be pleased with him), etc. Acting on the Divine advice:

Ask those who possess the Message, if you do not know.[1]

Even the eminent preservers (huffādh) of hadith and Qur'ān among the Companions would come to these distinguished personages for the solution of religious and legal problems and would subject their own understanding and interpretation to the interpretation of the Qur'ān and the hadith given by them.

Abu Hurairah (Allah be pleased with him) was one of those eminent Companions who were distinguished in the line of

---

[1] *Al-Anbiyā 21: 7.*

preserving and reporting the Holy Prophet (pbuh)'s traditions, and this is borne out by the large number of traditions reported by him and included in the books of hadith. But it is a fact well-known to the students of the history of Companions, that whenever someone was confronted with any religious or legal problem, he would not approach Companions like Abu Hurairah but those who were considered fuqahā (men of grasp and understanding). It was this latter class whose verdict (fatwā) was relied upon and whatever interpretation they gave to the sayings and actions of the Holy Prophet (pbuh) was accepted.

To make the distinction between the two categories of Companions practically clear, I may invite your attention to a famous hadith.

One day, the Holy Prophet (pbuh) went to a garden, in search of solitude, without telling anyone. Compelled by their intense love, the Companions became anxious after some time and started out in different directions to find him. Abu Hurairah succeeded in his attempt. He saw the Holy Prophet (pbuh) sitting on a well, in a quite spiritual repose and absorbed in communion with Allah. Finding Abu Hurairah by his side, the Holy Prophet (pbuh) turned towards him and said: "Whosoever recited there is none worthy. of worship but Allah' shall enter paradise." Abu Hurairah heard that heartening message and was overjoyed, feeling that the problem of salvation had become so simplified. He sought the permission to make it known to others. The Holy Prophet (pbuh) who was presumably in a special spiritual state at that time, replied: yes. Forthwith, Abu Hurairah started for the town. But he had not gone far when he met Umar, who himself was engaged in search of the Holy Prophet (pbuh). Abu Hurairah told him about the Holy Prophet (pbuh) and also mentioned the Holy Prophet (pbuh)'s saying just referred.

Umar asked him about his destination. Abu Hurairah informed him that he was going to the town to broadcast the Holy Prophet (pbuh)'s saying among the people. Umar said: "No! do not proclaim it." Abu Hurairah insisted that he would. Umar insisted that he should not. At last, both came to the Holy Prophet (pbuh). Umar implored: "O Messenger of Allah! If people will be informed of this hadith at the present stage of Islamic culture, they will' stick to its literal connotation that the recitation of the kalimah (article of faith) is enough for salvation and will leave Islamic actions". The Holy Prophet (pbuh) ' expressed his approval of Umar's point of view.

Now, this clearly shows that Islamic scholarship does not consist merely in the ability to read Arabic, but in the capacity to reach the inner depths of the teaching contained in the Qur'ān• and the hadith. Take, for instance, the Hadith in question. To recite the kalimah with the tongue is meaningless unless it expresses the corresponding conviction. And conviction means nothing less than submitting oneself to Allah's commands and the leadership of Holy Prophet (pbuh). It comprehends within itself the whole sweep of Islamic life. In those early days of Islam, the apprehension was justified that people might take to Holy Prophet (pbuh)'s Saying literally. Hence the Faqih-ul-Millat, the wise man of the community, Umar, about whom the Holy Prophet (pbuh) declared: "Verily, Allah manifested truth on the tongue of Umar," he did not consider it proper to acquaint the people with that Hadith at that time and the Holy Prophet (pbuh) approved his judgement.

In short, it was the principle followed by the Companions, that whenever they had to find out about some religious or legal problem, they would invariably approach those Companions for guidance who were considered to possess not only the knowledge of the words of the Qur'ān and the hadith but also superior insight and understanding and were thus entitled to guide others.

This principle was followed during the whole period of Righteous Caliphate. For the interpretation and execution of Islamic law, there was an advisory council which was composed of such Companions who were most capable in matters of religion and law. The Amir-al-Mu'minin was always the President of the Council and whenever there was a disagreement on some legal point between the members, it was his prerogative to give the final verdict.

Chapter 5

The Codification of Law

After the period of the Righteous Caliphate, the Islamic empire came under the control of monarch-caliphs, one of whom was Yazid, well-known as a despot and an unconscientious ruler. Moreover, the boundaries of the Islamic State were expanding fast.

In such a situation, there was every likelihood of arbitrary interpretations, heterodoxies, and heresies. Consequently, it became necessary to compile the Islamic law in a codified book form, classifying the laws and the bye-laws and clarifying the topics and the problems. The object was to enable every literate Muslim to know the law without taking the long and tedious route of going to the original sources, acquiring knowledge of a research-scholar level in the Qur'ān, the hadith and Islamic history in all its aspects, and attempting to discover every minute law and its deduction himself. This work of simplified and clear-cut presentation of the Islamic law was undertaken by those distinguished scholars and spiritual luminaries of Islam who, by their great qualities of head and heart, deserved to be considered the true successors of the Prophet, in the words of the hadith.

On the one hand, the Medinite scholar, the celebrated Imām Malik bin Anas started his Academy at Medinah, while on the other hand, Imām Abu Hanifa Nu`man bin Thābit applied himself to the same work at Kufa.

The system pursued at Imām Malik's Academy was that all the Islamic experts and scholars assembled there. There were no loud-speakers in those days. Hence, for the gathering, ten announcers had to be appointed during every discussion. The discussion used to commence each time with a statement from the Imām. That was broadcast to the gathering by the announcers. Then the general debate would start. Each individual scholar presented his opinion on the problem and quoted from the hadith literature in his support. Criticism and counter-criticism from all points of view would ultimately bring the assembly to favour and support a certain hadith on a certain problem. Thereafter, the heading was fixed and the hadith was entered under that heading. Thus, came into existence the well-known book, called Al-Muwaṭṭa' of Imām Malik, which presents one of the attempts at the codification of Islamic law.

The transfer of the capital of the Islamic empire from Medinah by the Umayyad rulers, brought Kufa and Syria into great prominence. Islamic learning became gradually centralized in that area and the Islamic legal activity of the whole empire became focalized there. To those parts came the best Islamic legal brains and the greatest men of religious learning, not only to fill the various governmental offices but also to add lustre to the centre of the empire.

The Academy of Imām Abu Hanifa was ta Kufa, incorporating the learning of some of the best Islamic brains of those days. Imām Abu Hanifa acted as the president, and Imām Muhammad and Imām Abu Yusuf worked as joint secretaries.

Several of the greatest Islamic scholars were present, and they were those who remembered not only thousands, but hundreds of thousands of the traditions of the Holy Prophet (pbuh). It was an age close to the Holy Prophet (pbuh)'s. We all know that Imām Abu Hanifa had received traditions from the second generation of Muslims. But it is also a fact that he received the knowledge of hadith from some of the Companions too. The system adopted in the Academy was to first classify the verses of the Holy Qur'ān under various topical headings and sub-headings. The whole hadith literature was then taken up. Each Hadith was examined thoroughly from all points of view, employing historical criticism as well as logical criticism. Ultimately, the issue under investigation was clarified, the legal form of the problem was agreed and the section of the law was entered in a classified form in the compilation. Musnad of Imām Abu Hanifa and Al-Muwaṭṭa' of Imām Muhammad are the books which represent that attempt at legal codification from the point of view of traditionists (muhaddithin). They are books of hadith arranged according to legal problems and giving the authority for each tradition mentioned therein.

It is well worth remembering that the Holy Qur'ān describes Islam as din. This word is usually translated as religion in English for want of a better single word.

The expression 'way of life' denotes the meaning better. Now, Islam comprehends two distinct elements, namely: (1) teachings relating to faith and belief, (2) teachings concerning various forms of Islamic practice. Those who attempted the classified codification of Islam took into consideration both elements. The first they described as theology (imaniyat), the second as Law. At the Academy of Imām Abu Hanifa, the compilation of the Islamic teachings falling under the first category was given the name of Fiqh-al-Akbar (or Higher Law), while the work falling in the second category has come to be described as fiqh in the general sense.

In the Fiqh-al-Akbar, all the articles of Islamic belief have been given in logical arrangement, so that everyone who wants to know his faith may refer to that handy book. Discussions relating to the sources and the arguments have been left out. This work was accomplished separately by other Imāms who wrote volumes in support of Islamic metaphysics and controverted the false teachings of the adversaries among philosophers. They dealt with all those problems exhaustively, so much so that ultimately, they succeeded in building up a whole new science - the science of dialectics or kalām. The Imāms of the schools of Ash`ariyyah and Māturidiyyah established their respective academies and rendered an immortal service to the cause of Islam. They systematized Islamic theological teachings and they built up· a treasure of philosophical and logical arguments which will always remain the pride of Islamic history. The book on aqā'id by Nasafi and its commentaries. are too well known. There are numerous others which the scholars of the Ash`ariyyah and Māturidiyyah schools wrote and in which they fortified ·the Islamic belief.

When we cast a glance at the other branch of fiqh which deals with our actions in reference to Allah as well in reference to our fellow-human beings, we find that the Academy of Imām Abu Hanifa compiled the source books of hadith known as Musnad of Imām Abu Hanifa and Al-Muwaṭṭa' of Imām Muhammad. These were, so to say, guide-books for the scientific codification of the law in a precise form.

But his work was not enough by itself. The principles of deduction had also be fixed up in the light of the method employed by the

Companions of the Holy Prophet (pbuh). Without such principles, the work of deducing the section of law from the Holy Qur'ān and the hadith was not possible. That important work could not be based on individual personal opinions of scholars, however great they might have been, but on principles which were grounded fully in the Holy Qur'ān and the Hadith and the guidance given by the Companions. It was a great task and it was accomplished under the name of Usul-i-Fiqh (i.e., Principle of Law). Today, there exist voluminous books on this subject. Among those which are taught in theological universities, Usul-i- Shāshi for the lower classes, and Nur-ul-Anwār for the middle classes are very well known.

It was solely on the foundations of the Holy Qur'ān and the hadith and the Principles of Law deduced from the Holy Qur'ān and the hadith that the science of Law was built. This science deals with the rules of ibādāt (categories of worship) and with the laws relating to the multifarious problems arising from human relations at various levels. The central figures, who engaged themselves in that work at the Academy of Imām Abu Hanifa, were three: Imām Abu Hanifa (President), Imām Muhammad and Imām Abu Yusuf, as scribes and joint secretaries. They were assisted and advised by nearly five hundred scholars of Islam, who were distinguished for their piety and learning.

It may be pointed out here that the function of Imām Abu Hanifa in that Academy was not that of a dictator. The method of work was not that he ordered a certain piece of law to be written down and it was written. It was not his opinion which guided the work. Nay, the method really was that the Book of Allah and the Holy Prophet (pbuh)'s sunnah were first investigated thoroughly for finding out the explicit ruling of Islam on a certain problem of law. The work of deducing the law was undertaken whenever the guidance was not explicit.

In that case the scientific objective and fixed principles of Law were the guide and not any subjective opinion or consideration. Every scholar had equal right to apply the principles. There were full-fledged discussions, criticisms, and counter-criticisms on every problem. The best and the most honest effort was made to come to a unanimous conclusion. If even then, there was any difference of opinion, the stand of Imām Abu Hanifah was preferred in some cases and the stand of Imām Muhammad and Imām Abu Yusuf in others. This was the democratic, honest, and impartial method of codifying the Islamic Law by the Academy of Imām Abu Hanifa.

In later times, the coming generations of scholars built up great edifices of law on those foundations. Thousands of books were written commenting upon and explaining the various aspects of that work. Today, this vast literature is a mine of information, capable of meeting every legal need of the Islamic world.

Were I to mention only the names of those numerous books which have been written in that connection, it would fill a volume. There are some that are more commonly-known, are taught in theological institutions, and have also been translated into Urdu, e.g. Quduri, Kanz-ud-Daqā'iq, Sharh Waqāyah, Hidāyah, Durr-e-Mukhtār, etc. Radd-ul-Mukhtār and Fath-ul-Qadir are handy books of reference for the muftis.

Usually, the books on Islamic Law which are in common use do not contain elaborate information as to sources and arguments. This leads some people to attack such books as dealing with the personal opinions of the Imāms. Nothing can be farther from truth. Books for practical day-to-day guidance of the general masses must quite naturally be simple and should contain nothing more than a bare and clear statement of the Law. Such books are always condensed forms of more elaborate compilations, where one can find the statement of the sources and the argument in full. As I have already explained, the work of the Imāms was simply to state those laws which are explicitly given in the Holy Qur'ān and the Holy Prophet (pbuh)'s sunnah and to discover those laws which are implicit there, and to state them accordingly. In fact, there is not a single law stated by the Imāms which is not based on the Qur'ān and the sunnah, and there is not a single deduction which was made without reference to the Qur'ān and the sunnah and the method of deducing employed by the Companions, who were directly taught and trained by the Holy Prophet (pbuh).

This makes it clear that the Ilm-ul-Fiqh is nothing but a systematic statement of the laws, explicit and implicit, found in the Holy Qur'ān and Holy Prophet (pbuh)'s Sunnah, and the titles of Fuqahā or mujtahids were given to those who performed that work.

If we employ our common sense for a while, we can easily realize that by the systematization of Islamic Law, the Imāms have laid the Muslim world under such a deep debt of gratitude for which no amount of expression of thanks can suffice.

Those great personalities of Islam were the people who had attained the pinnacle of possible perfection in theoretical knowledge, whose hearts were illumined with spiritual light, whose lives were embodiments of piety and fear of Allah, who had devoted years and years to the understanding of Islamic legal science, who worked first under the guidance of a teacher like Imām Abu Hanifa and, later, perfected the work in the same light. They knew the fact and they had absolute faith in it that as human beings, they had no right to create laws from their brains. They were fully conscious of the truth that Allah Alone has the right to make laws for His creatures -The Command is for none but Allah.[1]

They were aware that:

"If any do fail to judge by (the light of) what Allah revealed, they are (no better than) transgressors [2]"

Their work was simply to utilise the gift of higher understanding (tafaqquh) which Allah had given to them to systematise the laws given in the Qur'ān and the Sunnah, according to the requirements of the full-grown Muslim community.

This is the work which was performed by Imām Malik and his co-workers and pupils in Medinah and by Imām Abu Hanifa and his co-workers and pupils in Syria and Iraq. Later, Imām Shafi`i and Imām Ahmad ibn Hanbal performed the same work with the same honesty and erudition. These great Imāms rendered the fundamental service to Islam and left behind them a solid literature on Islamic Law, on which the mighty structure of Islamic administration was built. Muslims were the masters of their destinies for twelve centuries.

During this long period, it was the work of these Imāms which continued to feed Muslim progress and Islamic life, not only in

---

[1] *Yusuf 12: 40.*
[2] *Al-Mā'idah 5: 47.*

rituals and matters of worship, but also in all the conceivable aspects of politics, economics, state-law, international law, etc. Our whole past and present is a standing testimony to the consensus of Islamic learned opinion that truth is to be found in the four schools, i.e., Hanafi, Shafi`i, Maliki and Hanbali, and those who revolt against them revolt against the Book of Allah and the Sunnah.

This means that in the fundamental exposition of the Islamic Law, these schools have accomplished what was humanly possible from all aspects. The honest course for us is to follow that exposition in all the issues clarified therein.

If however, we are ever confronted with any issue, which comes into existence because of the growing complexity of human life, the course for us is, that those among us who are really capable of it because of their piety and sound learning, and not every Tom, Dick and Harry, should approach the Holy Qur'ān and the Holy Prophet (pbuh)' sunnah for light and should deduce the law from there, conforming all the time to the Islamically-based method followed and the path of investigation blazed by the great Imāms.

It is, indeed a great misfortune that some of our brothers feel today that they can equal, nay, even surpass the great Imāms based on their smattering of Islamic knowledge derived from faulty translations of the Holy Qur'ān and some petty English books on hadith, and that they can deduce the legal guidance from the Qur'ān and the hadith themselves. I wish they could cultivate more humility and could properly assess their true capacities.

In connection with the problem of discovering the Islamic guidance on some newly-created issue, I may cite an incident of my own life. Once some modern educated young men for the Osmania University of Hyderabad, Indica, came to me, presented to me several questions and demanded that I should, in each case, give a reply from the Holy Qur'ān. When I had done so, they asked me how could the Qur'ān supply guidance on any issue which did not exist at the time when fatwas revealed? As an instance, they asked me to state from the Qur'ān whether it was or not permissible for a Muslim to witness the play at the cinema. I told them that I had never been to a cinema and that I wanted first to know from them what it was. They told me how a plot is first fixed up, then a story is invented, then it acted by the actors and the acting is filmized and shown on the screen by means of electricity. I asked them not to relate a whole story but to give an appropriate definition. After a brief discussion, we agreed on defining a cinema performance as a play based on an invented tale. I, then, asked them whether they were ready to abide by the decision if the Qur'ān forbade them. They gave their definite promise. Then I read to them the following verse from the Qur'ān:

> "But there are, among men, those who purchase idle tales (or, those who spend money on the play based on tale), without knowledge (or meaning), to mislead men from the path of Allah and to hold it in ridicule: for such there will be a humiliating penalty.[3]"

All present bowed before the Qur'ānic verdict and repented as promised.

I have cited this incident to point out that the Holy Qur'ān is indeed the Book of perfect guidance. If anyone dives deep into its meanings, he can discover the guidance contained therein on every conceivable issue. But this insight comes only when one acquires specialized training in the schools of the mujtahid Imāms.

---

[3] *Luqmān* 31: 6.

Chapter 6

Ijtihad and Mujtahid

The island of Trinidad enjoys British administration and is governed by British law[1]. Those who wish to enter any such government service here which concerns itself with the administration of law are bound to qualify themselves in the knowledge of the British law. For instance, even he who is desirous of holding the job of a police sergeant must study the section of criminal law before he can be hired for the job. Thus, every Police Sergeant in the colony can claim to possess the knowledge of law.

But, can you ever conceive, that because of that knowledge of Law which a police sergeant might possess, the government can ever consider him eligible for the post of the Judge of the Supreme Court or that of the Attorney-General. If a sergeant could equal a Barrister-at-Law or an LL.D., the Lincoln's Inn and the Faculties of Law at the great Universities would not exist.

No one can be given the right of interpreting the man-made laws, which continue to change and to be amended from day-to-day, unless he is a fully qualified Barrister-at-Law, nay, unless he has mastered the higher History of Law, Social Psychology and Sociology, etc., and can stand up in the true sense a Doctor of Law. But, what a pity, that people can afford to believe that the work of Ijtihad, i.e., of interpreting the revealed Law of Allah and of deducing new laws from it, can be done by X, Y, Z. Such a monstrous suggestion simply staggers the imagination and it can possibly come only from those who have but a scant regard for Allah and His Law!

The word Ijtihad has been derived from the root jahd, and literally means striving with full exertion. In Islamic legal terminology, it denotes the endeavour of choosing, in the light of the Qur'ān and the sunnah, between two or more differing legal interpretations and of deducing from the Qur'ān and the Sunnah, any new rulings for meeting new legal situations. One who performs ijtihad is called a mujtahid.

The learned men of Islam have laid down certain qualifications in

---

[1] The lecture was given before the Independence of Trinidad in 1962.

the light of the Qur'ān and the sunnah, which a person must possess for acting and for being accepted as a Mujtahid. Shah Waliullah of Delhi (may Allah bless him) has mentioned those qualifications in detail in his celebrated book Hujjatullah-i-al-Baligha.

I may summarise them herein their minimum form especially for the benefit of those simple-minded brothers and sisters of mine who have been misled into the belief that they can act as mujtahids in their independent capacities. Let those whom the promptings of personal fancies lead them into posing as mujtahids without right, and who condemn the great services rendered by the Imāms simply because their hearts are gripped by un-Islamic things and they cannot bear the Islamic discipline systematized and codified by the latter; pause for a while in an attitude of just consideration and think. The following are the minimum reasonable qualifications, on the Islamic side, which a mujtahid should possess:

1. He should be an expert in Arabic language, literature, and philology, so that he may be able to decide properly between the different connotations of the same word.

2. He should be a high-class scholar of the Qur'ān, and his study of it should .be so extensive and intensive that whenever he must consider a given problem, he should be capable of keeping before his mind's eye the whole sweep of Qur'ānic thought and all the relevant verses.

3. He should have the traditions of the Holy Prophet (pbuh) in his memory, so that whenever he must focus his mind on any problem, he may have all the connected traditions, even those connected indirectly, before him clearly and vividly, to guide his thought process rightly and comprehensively.

4. He should further be an expert of the sciences of historical criticism (riwāyat) and logical criticism· (dirāyat), so that he may able to view the worth and connotations of   various traditions under study at the time, in their proper perspective.

5. Above all, he should possess piety and true Islamic character and his heart should be imbued with what the Qur'ān calls fear of Allah.

Now, my friends! if there is a person who claims to be a mujtahid, but who does not possess even one-tenth of these qualifications, what else can you say about him but that he is groping in the dark and what else can be the result of his stumbling but misguidance.

Shah Waliullah, the celebrated philosopher, theologian, legist, traditionist and commentator, before whose learning and piety bowed the Arab and non-Arab ulama, found all the qualities of a mujtahid in his person. Yet his sense of responsibility and fear of Allah withheld him from declaring his Imāmate and ijtihad and in all humility, he continued to regard himself as a follower (muqallid) of Imām Abu Hanifa's school of thought and continued to stress before the Muslims of India that they should stick to the Hanafi school, which had guided the Muslim governments for centuries and had been developed into a perfect system.

Qalaadah and taqlid are two related Arabic words. The word qalaadah means a rope or a chain which is bound to the neck of someone to make him follow behind. Taqlid connotes the act of following. As a religious term, it has reference to the fact that the servants of Allah, who are linked together by obedience to Allah, receive the commandments of Allah (ahkām) through such a chain.

That is, when someone says that he is the muqallid of Imām-e-Azam, it means that the chain through which he is receiving the Commands of Allah is that which passes through Imām-e-Azam to the Holy Prophet (pbuh) Muhammad. It never means that he is following the commands of Abu Hanifa. Nay, the Command is that given by Allah, the manner of grasp is that taught by the Holy Prophet (pbuh), the interpretation is that given by the Companions, the arrangement is that fixed by the Hanafi school. The work of the Ālim and the Mufti is to follow this chain, to acquire his knowledge of the Islamic Law in conformity with it and to guide the people in their legal affairs.

Suppose, today, someone enquires from me concerning some point of Islamic law. What shall I do? I have no right to give him some commandment on my own behalf or tell him something in the light of my own common sense. My function is merely to deliver the law which Allah has given and to guide the people on the basis of that revealed guidance. This function is also based on certain authority and certain qualifications. For instance:

1. If I am questioned about any problem relating to the Qur'ānic text, I can answer authoritatively, because I possess a continuous authority reaching up to the Holy Prophet (pbuh) Muhammad.

2. If I am questioned about any problem relating to the Qur'ānic exegesis or the sciences relating to the hadith literature, I can answer authoritatively, because I possess a continuous link of authority reaching up to the Holy Prophet (pbuh).

3. Similarly, if I am questioned about any problems relating to Islamic Law, in accordance with the Hanafi or Maliki or Shafi`i or Hanbali schools, I can answer authoritatively, because I possess continuous chains of authority passing through the four Imāms and reaching up to the Holy Prophet (pbuh).

I am here before you. My mode of life and my character is before you. The evidence of history about the authoritative learning and piety of my teachers is before you. The commands which I am delivering to you today and the teaching which I am explaining to you is not from me. It is the command and the teaching sent to humanity by Allah through the Holy Prophet (pbuh) Muhammad. In the field of Law, I know that every section of law which is found in Hidāyah, or Fath-ul-Qadir, or Durr-e-Mukhtār, or Shāmi, or any other similar book has been inserted there after utmost investigation and I am always ready to prove it.

After all, what these books of Islamic law (Fiqh) are? They are the hand-books detailing the Law which the Holy Prophet (pbuh) brought to humanity. They are the compendiums where each one of us can find a ready-made and clear-cut reply to his legal problem.

Even though it may prolong the discussion let me reiterate the argument I have been expounding so far. Let me state that:

1. The Holy Qur'ān is the basic book, the ground work of Islamic Law. The explanation and exposition of its teachings, in the light of the Holy Prophet (pbuh)'s traditions, is called Ilm-ul-Tafsir (or, the Science of Commentary). There exist numerous books on that subject, among which the better-known classics are: Tafsir Tabari, Tafsir Badawi, Tafsir Kashshāf and Tafsir Ma'alim-ut-Tanzil.

2. The explanation and detailed exposition of the Qur'ānic teachings by the Holy Prophet (pbuh), in his sayings and actions, forms the second basic source of Islamic

3. knowledge. Now that science which deals with the collection of those sayings and actions of the Holy Prophet (pbuh) is called the science of Hadith (ulum al-hadith). There are numerous books on that subject, the most well-known classical work being:

4. The Sahih-al-Bukhari, Muslim, Abu Daud, At-Tirmidhi, Ibn Majah, Muwaṭṭa' of Imām Malik, Musnad of Imām Abu Hanifa, Musnad of Imām Ahmad, etc., etc. There are several compendiums where the traditions have been arranged alphabetically, e.g. Kanz-ul-Ummāl and Bihār-ul-Anwār. There are some compilations· arranged in a third way, e.g., Ma'ani-ul-Athar.

5. The science which deals with the biographies of the reporters of traditions for the assessment of their worth, is known as the Science of Asmā-ur-Rijāl and there are many classical books relating to it.

6. The science which deals with the gradation of Traditions is known as the science of Usul-al-Hadith.

7. The science which deals with the Principles of Qur'ān and the Hadith is known as the Usul-al-Fiqh, and there are several classical works and numerous explanatory books on that subject.

When the laws are framed and deduced from the Qur'ān and the Hadith according to the rules of Usul-al-Fiqh, and they are arranged and systematized in the form of a Law-code, the science is called Ilm-ul-Fiqh.

There are a number of classics and numerous hand-books on that subject.

In mentioning this classification of Islamic sciences, my purpose is to give just an idea to my simple-minded brothers and sisters who are being thrown into confusion concerning the Islamic legal schools by certain unconscientious people, who wish to establish their own hegemony and leadership and hence they propagate all sorts of confusion. Some of them have their ulterior sectarian ends to gain. Most of them are ignorant of Islamic sciences and the safest way they can adopt for their leadership is that of the denial of the validity or the necessity of those sciences. Many of them are so unconscientious that they impute false motives to the Imāms, to call them any 'gods besides Allah' and to criminally impute shirk (polytheism) to most of the Islamic world which accepts the guidance of the Imāms in the matter of understanding the Islamic Law. Even a blind man can see how far they are right. Even the least intelligent person can grasp the element of blasphemy in their stand. Even the ordinary Muslim can understand that:

1. When the Commentator of the Qur'ān ponders over the verses of that Sacred Book, in accordance with the principles of language and grammar and in the light of the Traditions of the Holy Prophet (pbuh), he is doing nothing else than obeying the following command of the Qur'ān itself: Do they not then earnestly seek to understandthe Qur'ān.[2]

2. The scholar of hadith (muhaddith), when he applied himself to the understanding of the Holy Prophet (pbuh)'s sayings and actions, does so only in obedience to the Qur'ānic teachings: He who obeys the Messenger, obeys Allah.[3]

---

[2] Muhammad 47: 24.
[3] Al-Nisā 4: 80.

3. The scholar of Asmā-ur-Rijāl, when he carried out the work of examining the veracity of the reporters of the traditions, does so in conformity with the Qur'ānic principle of not accepting any report without exhaustive investigation: "You who believe! If a wicked person comes to you with any news, ascertain the truth, lest you harm people unwittingly, and afterwards become full of repentance for what you have done."[4]

4. The scholar who applies the science of Usul-al-Hadith for grading the traditions which are extant and for fixing up the categories of fard, sunnat, mustahab, permissible, non-permissible, partially permissible, etc., in the domain of practical injunctions, is only elaborating on the Qur'ānic command: And whatsoever the Messenger gives you, take it. And whatsoever he forbids abstain (from it).[5]

5. The scholar of Usul al-Fiqh fixes up the principles of Islamic law to elaborate the practical teachings of Islam for the believers, in obedience to the following Qur'ānic injunction:

   "If a party from every group remained behind, they could devote themselves to the task of gaining sound knowledge in religion.[6]"

6. The Imāms of Fiqh, when they systematize the legal injunctions of Islam in the light of Usul-al-Fiqh, do so merely to carry out the Qur'ānic injunction, which forms the remaining part of the verse, just quoted:

   "And that they may warn their folk when they return to them, so that they may beware."

   Those Imāms only further the mission of the Holy Prophet (pbuh)

---

4 Al-Hujurāt 49: 6.
5 Al-Hashr 59: 7.
6 Al-Tawbah 9: 122.

referred to in the following verse:

> "O Messenger! Make known that which has been revealed to you from your Lord.[7]"

When they teach Islamic guidance to the people, they do so in obedience to the Holy Prophet (pbuh)'s command:

> "Verily, let him who is present deliver the Message to him who is absent."

When the Imāms systematize the Islamic laws to save men from falling into errors and to make the path of their understanding smooth, they only act in accordance with the following Qur'ānic command:

> "Call unto the way of thy Lord with wisdom and fair exhortation, and reason with them in the better way. Lo! your Lord is Best Aware of him who strays from his way, and He is Best Aware of those who go aright.[8]"

Let us view the problem concretely. Suppose a Muslim goes to an Islamic scholar and questions him about the Islamic law on some point of ceremonial worship or on some point of human affairs, what do you think should be the procedure which that scholar should adopt? Do you think the following procedure can be adopted as the normal routine in all such cases? When a questioner comes to an ālim, and puts to him a query, the ālim concerned consults the Holy Qur'ān, studies it thoroughly for finding out the relevant verse or verses, shows the verse or verses to the questioner, explains the verse or verses in the light of linguistic, logical, or historical principles. Then he studies the whole hadith literature comprising hundreds of thousands of traditions, picks out the relevant traditions, examines their authenticity in the light of historical and logical criticism, decides the principles for preferring one hadith to

---

[7] Al-Mā'idah 5: 67.
[8] Al-Nahl 16: 125.

another, then he conjures the accurate legal form of the query, applies the knowledge he has obtained from the Qur'ān and the hadith in accordance with certain valid principles, formulates the Islamic law on the point and explains the whole procedure to the questioner and proves to him its validity from the point of view of the Qur'ān and sunnah. Then the questioner might feel that he had escaped taqlid and that he has received guidance direct from the Qur'ān and the sunnah. In fact, even with such a procedure, the enquirer or questioner has slipped into taqlid, for the knowledge he has obtained is through the medium of that scholar.

Even if you can consider such a procedure feasible in each and every case, do you think that every Maulvi is really capable of adopting and working according to that procedure? Does every Maulvi possess that vast learning and that deep insight necessary for the adoption of that procedure? Does every Muslim possess the understanding whereby he can associate himself in the scholarly endeavour of the Maulvi to be able to claim, even formally, that he has received the guidance directly from the Qur'ān and the Sunnah and has escaped taqlid?

Can the verdict of the Qur'ān be falsified when it says:

"Can the learned and non-learned be ever equal?"

Tell me, my friends, is it humanly possible for you to conform to the above-mentioned procedure as a normal and necessary routine?

And let me ask you, what do you do when you are confronted with any problem connected with the man-made law which governs your colony. When you have a law suit, do you call upon your barrister to explain to you all the background of the relevant sections of the law, their origin, their history, their different interpretations by legal authorities, the various rulings given by judges from time to time, so on and so forth? Well, you only explain the case to the barrister and discuss it with him and leave out all the above-mentioned questions as irrelevant.

Again, it is the function of the barrister to state the law and employ it and interpret it for pleading his case. Do you think that the government can accuse him on that basis of acting as a legislator and a law-giver? Or, do you think that the authors of law-books and commentators of law can be reasonably accused of taking the authority into their hands?

If the answer is in the negative, and it can only be in the negative, how can anyone accuse the Imāms of usurping the authority of Allah or His Prophet. Let me declare, and declare most emphatically, that if the Imāms took away the authority of anyone it was only the authority of those mischief-mongers who are always out to create confusion in the ranks of Muslims and of those half-educated people who, because of their self-conceit and other faults, like to pose as authorities to misguide people. The Imāms acted as the spokesmen of Allah and His Holy Prophet (pbuh) and whosoever follows their direction today actually follows nothing else but the guidance of the Qur'ān and the sunnah. The work of the Imāms confirms the fact that the religion (of Islam) is easy. Thanks to the great labours of the Imāms of tafsir, hadith and fiqh, today the knowledge relating to every department and every branch of the Islamic way of life is open to us, properly systematized and simplified, completely preserved and protected.

1. The Qur'ānic text is present, preserved to the very letter;
2. The commentary of the Qur'ān is present in bulky volumes;
3. The traditions of the Holy Prophet (pbuh) are present in books of hadith and siyār (biographies of the Holy Prophet (pbuh));
4. The literature on Asmā-ul-Rijāl is present to help us in examining the traditions;
5. Comprehensive books on principles of tradition and principles of law are present to make us understand the method of deducing laws from the Qur'ān and the sunnah;
6. Voluminous books on theological problems are present to guide us on beliefs (aqā'id);
7. Exhaustive books of law are present to guide us in matters of ceremonial, civil and criminal laws.

It is now for us either to practice Islam, which is the purpose for which Islam came, or to continue to waste our time in meaningless and new-fangled controversies.

There can be no doubt that the Holy Qur'ān is the store-house which contains all the knowledge we need. Similarly, the Holy Prophet (pbuh)'s traditions are the comprehensive treasure of guidance. If you want to find out a reply to any one of your problems from the Qur'an and the hadith, you can certainly find it in them. There you have the source and the fountainhead. But to discover it in that vast and deep treasure demands all your ambition, exertion, courage, and a thorough mastery of all those sciences which form the key to the unique treasure. Even if you can do that according to your insight, you might not still be sure of your conclusions.

The safest and the truest path for all is to seek help from those guide books which were built up by centuries of honest research, labour performed by the highest and the most pious intellects of Islam. Thus, if you have any problem relating to the meaning of the Qur'ānic verses, refer to the commentaries. If you wish to obtain information on any point relating to the Holy Prophet (pbuh)'s life, refer to the authentic books of hadith. If you want to be clear on any problem of Belief, refer to the classics of Ash'ariyyah and Māturidiyyah philosophers. If you want a reply to some problem relating to ceremonial or general law, refer to the books of Law according to the Hanafi, Maliki, Shafi`i and Hanbali schools. You will find your problems solved, your queries answered without much ado. You will discover the beauties of the codified Islamic law. I would advise you not to follow the example of the rat who found a piece of tamarind and started claiming that he was a full-fledged grocer.

Remember! the Holy Prophet (pbuh) prophesied for the later days in unambiguous terms that: "People will appoint ignorant persons as their (religious) leaders, who will give fatwā (legal verdict) without knowledge and will mislead their own selves as well as others. Beware of those mis-leaders!"[9].

About those very people who do not even know the Arabic language properly but who pose to be, not only muftis but, mujtahids, the Holy Prophet (pbuh) prophesied that they will be the

---

[9] Sahih Muslim 2673a, Book of Knowledge 47, Hadith 22.

"wolves in human dress" who are the hypocritical robbers of faith. They wear a crown of service to him.

Who whispers (evil) into the hearts of mankind among jinns and among men.[10]

They put on the mantle of hypocrisy, they utter the name of Islam with their lips but invite the people to all sorts of immoralities, nay, sometimes, to kufr itself.

Those evil geniuses are there, thanks to the ignorance of the Muslims. But the true scholars of Islam are always also present, to tear the mask from the face of evil - even as the Prophet of Allah truly prophesied:

"A party of my followers will continue to conclusively demonstrate the truth."[11]

In the fulfilment of this prophecy, numerous refulgent stars have appeared from time to time on the firmament of Islamic learning and have illumined the path of the followers of Islam. As for my humble self, I would consider it my good fortune if Allah Almighty counts me among their true students. As such I am always ready to render any service of which I may be capable.

Since my arrival in the island, I have found the Muslims entangled in certain controversies. The following are the questions which I have been asked to reply time and again.

1. Whether Isā (pbuh) was born without a father, or through the agency of a father?
2. Whether Isā (pbuh) died a natural death or is still alive?
3. Whether the mi'rāj (Ascension) of the Holy Prophet (pbuh) Muhammad (pbuh) was of a spiritual character or physical?
4. Whether a Muslim should read twenty rakā'ats in tarāwih or eight?
5. Is it permissible to hold the *Milād* assemblies?
6. Is it permissible to send blessings to the dead with Qur'ānic recitation?
7. Is it permissible for Muslim ladies to appear before

---

10 Al-Nās 114: 5-6.
11 Sahih Muslim 1923, Book of Government 33, Hadith 24.

strangers in revealing attires ?

I have been replying to the individuals on these points. But I have been asked to state the verdict of Islam in these matters for the benefit of the general Muslim public.

According to the argument which I have fully elucidated during the discussion of the codification of the Islamic law, my function is only to state the fatwā as it is found in the authoritative books of fiqh. That is the procedure which the Islamic world has been following.

Let me now state that, during the past thirteen centuries, most of the learned men of Islam have unanimously held, in the light of the Qur'ān and the sunnah, that:

1. Isā, (pbuh) was born without a father.
2. Isā (pbuh)was neither killed nor crucified, but Allah
3. saved him from the clutches of his enemies and has preserved him alive under His protection at a place He chose for him.
4. The Holy Prophet (pbuh) Muhammad (pbuh) performed the mi`rāj with his body which was light (nur) personified. This problem will be explained rationally during my lectures on miracles.
5. Keeping before him the sayings of the Holy Prophet (pbuh), which referred to the blessings to be obtained by increased amount of worship performed during the nights of Ramadān, and considering thoroughly the sunnah of the Holy Prophet (pbuh), Amir-ul-Mu'minin Umar (Allah be pleased with him!) fixed up twenty rakā`ats of congregational tarāwih prayers behind the Imām. Twenty rakā`ats of tarāwih are the sunnah of Umar (may Allah be please with him) and it is followed in obedience to the Holy Prophet (pbuh)'s command: "You should follow my sunnah and the sunnah of the righteous Caliphs."
6. To hold Milād assemblies and to recite the life of the Holy Prophet (pbuh) in conformity with the Holy Qur'ān and the hadith, is mustahab and mustahsan, i.e., a religiously good action.
7. To send blessings to the dead with Qur'ānic recitation is permissible and is an act based on the teaching of the Qur'ān and

the hadith.

8.   It is forbidden for Muslim ladies to appear before strangers dressed half-naked in the Western style.

This brief statement of Islamic guidance should not, however, mislead anyone to think that I am not prepared to argue out the fatwās which I might thus state. In fact, I am always ready to discuss any issue based on the original sources found in the Holy Qur'ān and the hadith, provided the person who wishes to discuss it with me has proper access to the technical knowledge necessary and comes to me as an honest student of the subject. Otherwise, to discuss the ins and outs of technical points with those who possess no technical knowledge of the Qur'ān and the sunnah would be as meaningless an act as discussing atomic physics with a school boy.

Unfortunately, certain sections of Muslims today have lost all sense of proportion. They may not even know the A B C D of the various Islamic sciences, but they have the courage to indulge in discussions of Islamic things with such a tone of authority as to make even the worse form of lunacy look grave. And not only can they pose as authorities, but they can also fight with fellow Muslims on the basis of their unwarranted and unauthorized views and can extend the fight to a limit where the community gets smashed up into pieces and becomes the laughing stock of the enemies of Islam. What is still more pitiable is that all this fight of the ignorant and petty "mujtahids" revolves mostly around problems and issues which have no relation to the mission of Islam or the progress and stabilization of the Muslim community.

Here I might recall to your minds an incident of history which depicts very well the condition of these "friends" of Islam.

Before the Islamic conquest, Constantinople was the seat of the Byzantine Church and a great centre for Christian controversies. Fighting among themselves on petty issues relating to ceremonials and the like, had become the pastime of the Christian clergy. They were engaged in it during that night also when the armies of Muhammad the Conqueror were crossing the Bosphorus. The most eminent among them were present in the beautiful church of St. Sophia and a heated discussion was in progress. The issue was whether the bread to be used in the feast of Eucharist should be leavened or unleavened. The fury of the debaters rose ultimately to such a pitch that they tore off the robes of each other. Everyone had in mind to vanquish his opponent, not only in argument, but also physically.

In the meantime, the armies of Islam broke through the fortification of the town. The Byzantine empire came to an end. The Byzantine Church also disappeared in due course. The church of St. Sophia where the bishops fought on that petty issue so ferociously, became the house of Islamic worship. Not only that petty controversy, but Christianity itself was wiped out.

I must make this admission, though I must do so with a very sad heart, that I find the Muslims in the same unenviable position today which characterised the Byzantine Christians of those days. Muslims have lost all their past glory. They are virtually existing on the keg of a dynamite.

The antagonistic forces are fully busy in liquidating their spiritual and moral heritage. The very fundamentals of Islam are under fire. The organised movements of irreligion and immorality, which stand for destroying and wiping out religion as such, are attacking the Muslim religious life also with full force. Vast Muslim populations in Central Asia, Transcaucasia, Eastern Europe and China have been engulfed by atheistic Communism. Other Muslim populations are also suffering under the stress of the materialism-ridden modernism.

Such an all-round catastrophe necessitates that Muslims should stand united like a solid rock and should concentrate on the fundamental spiritual and moral issues confronting them. And not only this. They should invite the whole world of religion to join with them in fighting the organised menace of irreligion.

But, instead of this, there are certain persons who are never tired of raising petty issues for dividing Muslims and of wasting their energies. Such persons have, of course, their own axe to grind. What their actions mean to Islam, they do not care. It is, however for all sincere Muslims to see that they do not fall into the snare and do not allow themselves to be misled into wasteful pursuits.

Before I conclude, I pray that Almighty Allah may bless the

Muslims with the right understanding so that they may be able to distinguish the right from the wrong and to save themselves from pernicious influences. Ameen!

Appendix

Mawlānā Abdel Aleem Siddiqui: Man and Mission

by Abdul Kader Choughley

The renewed global and national networking of Islamic organisations and revivalist movements has its origins in the late nineteenth and early twentieth century. From Jamaluddin Afghani's Pan-Islam to Mawlānā Siddiqui's dynamic concept of tabligh, the Islamic reawakening in its varied forms has shaped the Islamic discourse of *islāh*[1] (reform), which is based on the *salf al-sālih*[2] (earliest representatives of Islam) presentation.

The paucity of literature on Mawlānā Siddiqui's biography has limited the scope for the critical evaluation of his contributions to Islamic thought. Apart from the overstrained accounts which accentuate a distinct sectarian bias, other biographical sketches are generally reproduced and repackaged from a single source to promote the preconceived profile of this eminent scholar. Fortunately, the biographical account and other articles on Mawlānā Siddiqui by his successor, Mawlānā Ansari[3] are considered reliable sources as they provide an overview of his contributions, which are corroborated by documents and materials contained in magazines and newspaper articles related to the period under study.

Likewise, Mawlānā Siddiqui's monographs and published lectures are useful guides to reconstructing, albeit briefly, his life and times. His unassuming personality and aversion for publicity were inextricably linked to the Islamic ethos he rigorously followed. His *taqwā* (Allah-consciousness) was his beacon light which illumined his radiant personality. In sufi terms, *fanā* (absorption in divine love)[4]

---

[1] Abdul Kader Choughley, *Fazlur Rahman Ansari: Life and Thought* (Springs, 2012), 26-34.

[2] Fazlur Rahman Ansari, "Shah Abdul Aleem Siddiqui: The Roving Ambassador of Islam" in *The Muslim Digest:* Jan/Feb 1996, 65.

[3] The title is used interchangeably for Dr Ansari in the study.

[4] The types of *fanā* in relation to *tasawwuf* are succinctly discussed in Amatullah Armstrong, *Sufi Terminology: The Mystical Language of Islam* (Kuala Lumpur, 1995), 46-

permeated the spiritual disciplines which he internalised in his daily life. In his view, spirituality[5] formed the core message of the Islamic teachings. Therefore, an uncompromising faith and committed practice to the Islamic principles were the criteria for a believer's success in both worlds.

Mawlānā Siddiqui argued that laxity, for example, had the baneful effect on the proper understanding of the Islamic teachings. His standpoint is instructive as the following example shows:

Let me give you an important warning: Beware! You have a spiritual treasure during Ramadan. Take care! Just as thieves of material riches are always planning to rob people, similarly, the baser self and the devil are the thieves who are on the lookout for stealing the spiritual assets. Today is the day of Eid. You are in the midst of well-earned rejoicing. The doors of Allah's unbounded Mercy are wide open. The breeze of divine forgiveness is blowing. But beware of Satan's mischief. The wine shops and gambling houses are also open. The immoral attractions of the cinema are also here. The half-naked physical attractions are out on the roads with their immoral enhancements. Be on your guard! Save the delicate glass of faith and piety from the deceptive attacks of evil. Protect the labour you have made during the days and nights of Ramadan.[6]

Biographical Sketch

A synoptic overview of Mawlānā Siddiqui's manifold contributions is provided by Mawlānā Ansari (d. 1974), an erudite scholar and leading figure in the Islamic resurgence movement of the twentieth century. As Mawlānā Siddiqui's successor and private secretary, Mawlānā Ansari imbibed his missionary fervour through the establishment of the Aleemiyah Islamic Institute (Karachi, Pakistan), serving as the link between the traditional and progressive Islamic thought. His major writings show an unmistakable

---

47.

[5] In the study, the term spirituality is loosely associated to *ruhāniyat*.
[6] Extracts from the Eid message delivered in 1950 in Port of Spain (Trinidad). The theme of moral regeneration resonates in his speeches which he delivered in major cities around the world during his tabligh tour.

influence of Mawlānā Siddiqui's tabligh vision.[7]

The following biographical sketch is extracted from several articles written by Mawlānā Ansari and covers the multifaceted contributions of Mawlānā Siddiqui. It also demonstrates the unrelenting efforts of a *dā'i* striving to establish unity (*ittihād*) among the divided *ummah*; to restore the credibility of Islam as a civilisational force, and more importantly, reinforce the universal values of morality and tolerance shared by other faith-based communities. The personal narrative reveals the inner aspects of a *muballigh* committed to the Islamic ideal: *service to humanity*.

Early Years

Mawlānā Siddiqui was born on 3 April 1892 in Meerut (India). He was a direct descendant of the first Caliph of Islam, Abubakr Siddiq. Endowed with unusual intelligence and exceptional memory, Mawlānā Siddiqui commenced his education at the early age of three years and devoted himself to the acquisition of Islamic learning. Thereafter, he completed his studies in *Dars i-Nizami*[8] at the Madrasah Arabiah Qawmiyah, Meerut, at the age of sixteen. But the desire to understand the modern problems of mankind and to reach out the message of Islam to the world at large, urged him to acquire modern education as well.[9]

As regards his Islamic studies, he did not discontinue them even while pursuing modern education. In fact, he continued with his studies till many years after he had entered the field as an Islamic scholar and amassed further knowledge in Qur'ānic exegesis (*tafsir*), hadith, *tasawwuf* and *Fiqh* in Makkah and Madinah through discussion and interaction with the leading Islamic scholars of the day.

---

[7] See Choughley, *Fazlur Rahman Ansari: Aligarh Years.*

[8] The *Dars-i-Nizami* which is associated with 'ulama of Lucknow was aimed at fostering an intellectual tradition in the period of political instability. The curriculum defined Islamic learning at the Islamic higher institutions. See Said Rafiq, Islami *Nizām i-Ta'lim* (Karachi, 1956).

[9] The 'ulama's response to modern education was influenced by colonialism. Politcal factors inhibited a positive outlook towards learning English and scientific disciplines. See Aziz Ahmed, *Islamic Modernism in India and Pakistan: 1857-1964* (London, 1967), 22-23.

As an erudite scholar he augmented his studies at the well-known Islamic libraries in the Arab world. He also benefited from the sufi masters such as Shaykh Ahmad al- Shams of Morocco, Shaykh al-Sanusi of Libya, Mawlānā Abdul Bāqi of Farangi Mahal and Mawlānā Ahmad Rāda Khan of Bareily[10].

Choice of Career

With the formal completion of education, various professions were open to him for earning his livelihood.[11] He was employed by the reputed firm of Haji Mohammad Husain Seedhi as a manager in Mumbai towards the close of 1918. Very soon he proved himself to be more than a match for the position and rose to be a partner. But he had been there hardly for a year when his restless soul took him to Islam's Holy Land (*muqaddas*) on his first pilgrimage (*hajj*). From there he returned with the decision to devote himself primarily to the moral and religious upliftment of humanity.

Spiritual Discipline

The atmosphere to which Mawlānā Siddiqui was exposed was saturated with spirituality and enviable scholarship. His mother was a deeply pious lady, while his father, Mawlānā Abdul Hakim Siddiqui, was not only a versatile scholar and a high-class poet but also a sufi of eminence.[12]

Being the youngest child and endowed with extraordinary talents, his

---

[10]For a biographical account of these scholars, the following books may be consulted: Nicola Ziadeh, *Sanusiyah: A Study of the Revivalist Movement in Islam* (Leiden, 1983); Francis Robinson, *The 'Ulama of Farangi Mahall and Islamic Culture in South Asia* (Delhi, 2001), Usha Sanyal, *In the Path of the Holy Prophet* (Oxford, 2008). Cf. *Anwār i-Rizā*, 96.

[11] Mawlānā Siddiqui had completed his B.A. in Meerut Islamia College. Likewise, he completed another course in Punjab University, which deepened his understanding of Arabic literature and Persian. His law degree in Allahabad University is also mentioned. See *Anwār i-Rizā*, 171-2.

[12] A specimen of his poems devoted to the personality of the Holy Prophet (pbuh) is emblematic of his high - ranking position in *tasawwuf*. See Qadri, *Azim Muballigh-i-Islam*, 55.

father held him in great affection and kept him close to himself and transmitted to him the blessings of his personality until he was nearly twelve. His initial training in *tasawwuf* was under his elder brother, Mawlānā Ahmad Mukhtar Siddiqui[13] from whom he received the *ijazah* (authority) in several great sufi orders (*silsilahs*).[14]

Spirituality thus became the marked feature which distinguished Mawlānā Siddiqui's life from the lives of many a religious leader, even as the combination of Western education with Islamic learning was his sign of distinction. Indeed, spiritual purification and illumination tempered with the moral, social and political salvation of humanity remained his mission throughout his life.

Oratorical Excellence

It has been said that orators are born and not made and it was literally true in the case of Mawlānā Siddiqui because he delivered his first public speech at the Jam'i mosque of Meerut at the age of nine. It must be noted that during his youth he had already made his mark as a successful public preacher (*khatib*) which earned him international fame decades later. An instance in point were his public lectures in Tokyo at several prestigious universities. As Professor

N.H. Berlas wrote from Tokyo:

> ... [for] a fuller appreciation one must hear Mawlānā Siddiqui from the platform. One is sure to be charmed like the audience here by his magnetic personality and oratorical powers, his loud and impressive but musical voice and splendid delivery.[15]

As an engaging conversationalist and as a charming orator, he was

---

[13] The contributions of Mawlānā Ahmad Mukhtar Siddiqui to tabligh in several Muslim countries including Burma (Myammar), in particular, have not been fully examined. Likewise, his political activities have received a brief mention.

[14] The spiritual lineage is provided in Umair Siddiqui, *The Roving Ambassador of Islam* (Karachi, 2011), 95-6.

[15] Abdul Aleem Siddiqui, *Cultivation of Science by the Muslims* (Karachi, n.d.).

equally at home in Urdu, Arabic, English and Persian[16] and used the first three languages during his numerous tours in different parts of the world.

The capacity to express himself according to the intellectual temperament of his listeners was Mawlānā Siddiqui's great asset and he employed it with equal mastery in his lectures before learned societies[17] as well as during his missionary tours among the indigenous people of the African hinterland.

Spiritual Work

With these qualities of head and heart together with his accomplishments, Mawlānā Siddiqui resolved in 1919 to devote himself purely to spiritual work as a *muballigh* of Islam. It was not a new decision, however, because he had nurtured it in his heart for years. In fact, he wrote a poem while still a boy which proved in later years to be prophetic. An English rendering of two of its couplets is given hereunder:

My heart yearns to show its bleeding scars. Wrought by the spiritual perversions of man
And to teach everyone on earth the Laws. This is my yearning and this is my aim. This is my intention and this my claim. With this, I yearn to scan the globe
And deliver to humanity the message of hope.[18]

The twin concept of humanity and hope were the ideals he cherished and through which he strove to highlight Islam's universal message. The decision once made was irrevocable in spite of the hardships which it entailed and the travels once commenced did not

---

[16] Mawlānā Siddiqui was also conversant in Japanese and Swahili, which facilitated his mission to these countries.

[17] *The Forgotten Path of Knowledge* is an instance in point.

[18] Mohamed, *The Roving Ambassador of Peace, xxiv Cf. The Muslim Digest:* 1996. These articles are generally reproduced in several magazines.

cease until virtually his final journey from this world. Even his last remains were not buried in his hometown but in the far-off city of Madinah. As a spiritual pilgrim, Mawlānā Siddiqui visited Makkah and Madinah several times, while as the Flag-bearer of the spiritual rearmament of mankind, he travelled to different regions of the world continually for forty years, returning to his family only for short breaks. This was remarkable in the field of tabligh.

Countries Visited

The countries he visited during those travels - many of them repeatedly were: Myanmar, Malaysia, Indonesia, Thailand, Vietnam, China, Japan, Philippines, Sri Lanka, Mauritius, Reunion, Madagascar, South Africa, Mozambique, Kenya, Tanzania, Uganda, Belgian-Congo, the Hijaz, Egypt, Syria, Palestine, Jordan, Iraq, France, Britain, West Indies, Guyana, Suriname, the United States and Canada.[19]

To travel for forty years is in itself a mighty feat of endurance. These strenuous journeys were undertaken by a spiritual pilgrim who gave to his spiritual labours sixteen to eighteen hours a day.[20] When we probe into his activities, and when we look at the many societies and institutions with diverse functions which he founded or inspired, the hundreds of converts who received the light of Islam through him, the hundreds of thousands of Muslims belonging to different races who were elevated through his preachings, we get an inkling into the greatness of this man.

His International Work

The following paragraph is a poignant description of Mawlānā Siddiqui's *jihād* which was synonymous with his tabligh endeavours:

---

[19] Several of these countries have been renamed in order to discard their colonial past. For example, Belgian Congo was a Belgian colony from 1908 to 1960. The former colony adopted its present name, the Democratic Republic of Congo.

[20] In his early tabligh tours, Mawlānā Siddiqui was exposed to enormous challenges as the modes of transport were limited. The hurdles included rationing in the aftermath of World War One. Under these bleak circumstances, he was not deterred to spread the message of Islam in the remote areas of the world.

Mawlānā Siddiqui's message of Allah- realisation *(taqwā)*, of moral regeneration and of spiritual revival penetrated millions of hearts. His visits everywhere gave new impetus to the religious fervour of the people. His work transformed sandy deserts of spiritual inertia into green orchards of moral dynamism. His spiritual magnetism purified the social conscience of the people and in the wake of his visits sprang up orphanages for the helpless youth, infirmaries for the destitute, hospitals for the suffering humanity, educational institutions for the propagation of knowledge, assemblies for the dissemination of spiritual discipline, mosques for the worship of Allah, missionary societies for the propagation of the Divine message, interfaith organisations for the consolidation of religious forces against the onslaught of materialism and atheism and Muslim unity boards for the creation of harmony among Muslims.[21]

The spiritual content of his mission gave renewed meaning to the Islamic reawakening discourse. In fact, the gamut of activities to which he was associated, underscored his commitment to the Islamic cause for which he devoted his life. It was, therefore, not surprising that he was instrumental in the establishment of institutions ranging from missionary societies to orphanages. This realisation was a profound commitment to conscientise the *ummah* on its revolutionary mission to serve humanity.

Service to the Cause of Pakistan

When Muslims in India launched their struggle for self-determination and for the creation of Pakistan,[22] Mawlānā Siddiqui who had already contributed to the cause of Muslim politics during the Khilafat movement put all his weight in favour of the struggle. He went even so far as to snatch one year from his spiritual work and to travel to the world for aligning the hearts of the Muslim world with the righteous cause of the Indian Muslims.

Mawlānā Siddiqui, who was perhaps the most suitable man for this

---

[21] Ansari, "Abdul Aleem Siddiqui's Role in Modern History" in *The Muslim Digest*: September 1959, 12.

[22] On the ʿulamaʾ's contributions to the Pakistani cause, see Qureshi, *Ulema in Politics*, 339-70.

purpose because of his fluency in Arabic and his contacts with Arab leaders, realised the urgency of the situation and undertook to visit Egypt, Palestine, Lebanon, Syria, Trans-Jordan (now Jordan) and Iraq. In Egypt, he stayed with his friend Shaykh Hasan al-Banna (d.1949), founder of the Muslim Brotherhood (*Ikhwān al-Muslimin*).[23] From there he contacted the Egyptian intelligentsia, media and statesmen and convinced them of the just cause of the Indian Muslim struggle. There were other ʿulama from different theological (*maslak*) backgrounds who also contributed to the Pakistani cause.

Quest for Harmony

Fragrant sweetness was the keynote of Mawlānā Siddiqui's life. True peace - peace with Allah and peace with man - was his watchword; harmony between nations and races and parties was his aim; and the spiritual rearmament of humanity was his mission. Strife was alien to his nature and so were narrow-mindedness, bigotry and sterile religiosity. Throughout his long career as an international religious leader, there was no occasion when even his critics could point out a flaw in his religious personality[24] or in his sincerity and moral earnestness.[25]

His position as a messenger of peace on behalf of Islam did not, however, mean compromise. He was a staunch believer in the absolute truth of Islam, in its great mission, in its ennobling principles and in its elevating practices. What he was deadly against was baseless strife founded on egotism and not on altruism.

---

[23] For his biographical account see I.H. Husaini, *The Muslim Brethren: The Greatest of Modern Muslim Movements* (Beirut, 1956); Brynjar Lisa, *The Society of the Muslim Brothers in Egypt* (Reading, 1998).

[24] A detailed discussion appears in his *Quest for True Happiness*. See Siddiqui, *Dimensions of Islam* (Durban, 2005), 15-28.

[25] In the early years of his mission Mawlānā Siddiqui was subjected to a tirade of misrepresentations by his critics. See Siddiqui, *The Clarion Call*, 30-31. This was understandable in view of his global profile that transcended sectarian affiliations.

Goodwill and Harmony

Mawlānā Siddiqui struggled not only to remove the differences and antagonisms existing between Muslims rooted in political oppositions, social dissensions, and juristic differences (*ikhtilāf*)[26] but also to bring about understanding and goodwill between Muslims and non-Muslims.

His writings reflected his non-sectarian outlook; his preachings acquired the character of presenting Islam on the fundamental level, to which all his published English lectures bear witness, and to avoid all inter-school theological bickering. He made a positive effort to bring about goodwill and harmony. His participation in the establishment of an organisation, under the presidentship of Muhammad Ali Allouba Pasha of Egypt with Dr. Shawarib as its Secretary- General was significant. The organisation was named as *Taqrib bayn al-madhāhib Islami* (Society for the promotion of harmony between Muslim Islamic schools of thought).[27]

Society for the Promotion of Interfaith Cooperation

Mawlānā Siddiqui's yearning to see peace and goodwill established on earth was well known to everyone who came into contact with him. He carried in his heart the conviction that peace is unattainable by modern humanity unless every man and woman strove for spiritual rearmament.

With this end in view, Mawlānā Siddiqui initiated in 1949 a movement among the leaders of different religions in Singapore: Muslim, Christian, Jewish, Buddhist, Hindu, Sikh, etc. His sincerity of purpose and persuasive eloquence succeeded in opening a new chapter in religious history.[28] A society known as The Inter-Religious

---

[26] Mohamed, *The Roving Ambassador of Peace*, xxi.

[27] A similar effort was initiated by Shaykh Mahmud (d. 1963) of Egypt. See Kate Zebiri, *Mahmud Shaltut and Islamic Modernism* (Oxford, 1993), 24-6, 172. Cf. Ansari, "Muhammad Abdul Aleem Siddiqui ki Dini khidmāt ki Mukhtsar Ta'aruf" in *The Minaret*: April 1996, 30.

[28] Qadri, *The Greatest Propagator of Islam*, 63-5.

Organisation (IRO) and composed of eminent leaders of different religions was formed to realise these objectives.

Personal Character

The very first thing that struck everyone who came into contact with him was the profound charm of his personality, which created a sense of awe and respect.

His unassuming character was reflected in his sincerity, independence and self-respect. This independence, however, never took the form of haughtiness or arrogance. His humility touched the hearts of thousands of people from all walks of life. He was ever polite, ever sweet, ever persuasively eloquent, and independent of all ulterior considerations and dependent on principles alone. This gave him dignity and personal self-respect.

Cheerfulness in adversity and reliance in Allah were the hallmarks of his exemplary character. He was at his best when confronted with obstacles, and he possessed a special aptitude for undertaking tasks for which he possessed apparently no material resources. Whatever gifts his very close friends presented to him with love and humility, he spent them most liberally in the way of Allah.

In his daily interaction, Mawlānā Siddiqui personified the true meaning of consciousness of duty. This trait of character was most conspicuous in his personality and the guiding force of his life. For instance, when he started his memorable world tour (1949-1950), it gave him a unique distinction in the history of Islam because he (and Mawlānā Ansari) was the first Muslim missionary to have performed it.[29] His physicians advised him complete rest in view of his delicate state of health. Not only was he physically weak at that time but had also already lost the sight of one eye while the other eye also was suffering from cataract, but those considerations could not deter him. "This body of mine is a trust from Allah," he told his remonstrating physicians, "and is meant to be exhausted in Allah's way. How, therefore, can I suspend my activity even for a day for

---

[29] There were several scholars who made pioneering efforts of tabligh in the West. However, the scope of their tabligh was limited. See, Muhammad Mojlum Khan, *Great Muslims of the West: Makers of Western Islam.* (Leicester, 2017).

considerations of bodily comfort. No, gentlemen, that is not possible."[30]

Demise

There are two noteworthy factors which stand out in connection with Mawlānā Siddiqui's demise:

- He died while in harness, remaining active to the cause of his mission practically up to the last day, although before his death he had been seriously ill for nearly one year.
- He died and was buried in Madinah, which is an enviable blessing of Allah for every righteous Muslim. His death occurred at such a time of the year when Muslims from all over the world assemble at Madinah after the *hajj*. He had served the cause of Islam all over the world. He was Islam's world-class missionary. And Allah, in His infinite mercy, blessed him with a world congregation for his funeral prayers. Muslims from far and near came and paid their last respects to him.[31]

Major Contributions

Wherever Mawlānā Siddiqui went, both laymen and intellectuals among non-Muslims were inspired to enter the fold of Islam through his inspiring lectures. He wrote about twenty books in Arabic, Urdu and English. He took an interest in world politics generally and Muslim politics particularly. On his own initiative he advocated the cause of Pakistan in the Arab world and other Muslim countries. He moved for the elimination of the unjust imposition of the *hajj* tax, which the Saudi government reduced after protracted negotiation when they recognised his moral force.

Mawlānā Siddiqui's mastery of languages lent charm and beauty to

---

[30] Mohamed, *The Roving Ambassador of Peace*, xvi.
[31] Ansari, "His Eminence Muhammad Abdul Aleem Siddiqui Al- Qaderi: A Pioneer 'World Missionary" (Adapted) in *The Minaret*: May 1996, 8-18.

his thoughts and ideas. His eloquence was evident during his lectures before such learned societies as the Royal Asiatic Society of Shanghai and the Oriental Culture Society of Japan, as well as during his lecture travels to the African continent. Whether on the public platform or in private conversation, Mawlānā Siddiqui's exposition of contemporary problems was invariably marked by such lucidity, profundity and spiritual dynamism which were unrivalled. He belonged to both the worlds - traditional and modern; he was equally well- acquainted about the past, the present and the future; and he was equally impressive among the conservatives and the modernists. He was traditional in the sense that he carried on his venerable shoulders the responsibility and the obligation of delivering to humanity the message which Allah granted to the Prophets and Messengers in the different parts of the world. At the same time, he was modern in the sense that he possessed the ability to expound that message in contemporary idiom. He believed that science and religion, far from being antagonistic, are complementary to each other and can be optimally pursued in the best interest of mankind.

In sum, Mawlānā Siddiqui's tabligh vision transcended the traditional understanding of this term; his missionary spirit focused on the unity of the Muslim *ummah* which regrettably was fragmented into sectarian groupings. Disunity had weakened the spirit of brotherhood *(ukhuwwah)*, the bedrock of Islam's universal message. For forty years he strove to perpetuate the idea that the unity of the *ummah,* embedded in the primary sources of Islam, was the benchmark of Muslim progress across the world.

For forty years Mawlānā Siddiqui's travels extended to major countries of the world. The modes of travels were hazardous in several countries especially in Africa which were under colonial rule. Flights between India and European countries including USA were in their initial stages; however, perseverance was his inner strength which he drew from the Qur'ān and the Prophetic model.

With no organised financial backing, with apparently insurmountable difficulties constantly facing him, with broken health and continuous illness and with many to criticise and few to cooperate, he had to tread this lonely path. Under these adverse conditions, he maintained an admirable composure which imparted a spiritual glow to his every action. With his battle-cry: *Back to the Qur'ān and the sunnah*, his watchword: *the unity of Islam* and his conviction that *"[the] more religious Muslims become, the better will they succeed in solving all their problems,"* he fought against the forces of disruption and disintegration, creating harmony between the forces of conservatism, sectarianism and modernism.[32]

In the wake of his endeavours came a new awakening, a fresh consciousness and a stronger will to work, and these factors resulted in the establishment of missionary societies, youth movements, organisations of the ʿulama, educational institutions, mosques, orphanages, magazines and newspapers. And this new awakening captured the minds of all classes of Muslim society. Before the greatness of his work as also of his personality bowed princes and governors, judges and lawyers, students and professors, business magnates, bureaucrats and professionals from diverse backgrounds. His disciples in the 1950s exceeded nearly one hundred thousand souls while his admirers and friends numbered by the millions.

Survey of Writings by Mawlānā Siddiqui

Mawlānā Siddiqui's works must be understood in the context of historical developments in Egypt and the Indian subcontinent during the late nineteenth and early twentieth century. Both countries under British rule were exposed to a sustained form of Western civilisation.[33] Alongside this incursion of new intellectual thought was the rise of reformist Islam[34] challenging the ritualistic Islamic practices. Thus, the bold step to refer to the sources of Islamic authenticity was resisted by the polemical writings from those ʿulama who vigorously identified themselves with ritualistic Islam. The

---

[32] See Choughley, *Fazlur Rahman Ansari: Life and Thought* (Springs, 2012).

[33] For a detailed discussion about Western civilisation's influence on the Muslim world, see Francis Robinson, *Islam, South Asia and the West* (New Delhi, 2007), 99-123.

[34] According to Mazheruddin Siddiqui, the Muslim modernists were largely interested in the reconstruction of the Muslim society. Their worldview covered the intellectual, social and political bases which brought them into confrontation with the traditional ʿulama. See Siddiqui, *Modern Reformist Thought in the Muslim World* (Islamabad, 1982), 1-40.

tendency to confinate Islam in its pristine form with cultural accretions was very much evident in the Indian subcontinent. Other Muslim countries, too, were exposed to different forms of religious syncretism.

Again the period under discussion brought in its wake a cadre of the Muslim modernists - `ulama and scholars- who critically reviewed the legacy of Islam through the lens of Western civilisation. It would, therefore, be not surprising that the `ulama establishment, scholars of traditional Islam, were pitted against the Muslim modernists who were unequivocal in their condemnation of *taqlid*[35] and advocated new strands of Islamic intellectual thought. In view of the religious autonomy enjoyed by the `ulama over the centuries, the battle lines of Islam and Western civilisation were drawn. Instead of appropriating the technological benefits of the West, the `ulama perceived these as an encroachment to Islam's faith and practice. As a corollary, the study of English was vehemently frowned upon as it was considered the bastion of Western art and culture. Ishtiaq Qureshi's assessment of the conflicting relationship between the `ulama and the colonial society is revealing:

The European powers saw danger in this doctrine and the word Pan-Islam became obnoxious to all imperialists, not only because they did not want to let go what they held, but also because they were determined to grab more. It was not easy to hide this sentiment which was sometimes expressed openly, and sometimes clothed in ambiguous and less offensive words. With the growth of European power, European languages came to be studied in varying degrees in the various Muslim countries and the subcontinent was no exception. An access to European journals, reports and books gave the Muslims an insight into Western policies and ambitions. The knowledge percolated to the masses and the `ulama, who had mostly, almost universally, abstained from learning any European language.[36]

---

[35] The debate about the validity of *taqlid* (adherence to the authoritative explanation by the four Imams) continued unabated in the twentieth century. Mawlānā Siddiqui's exposition of *taqlid* is cogently expressed in his *The History and Codification of Islamic Law* (Karachi, n.d.).

[36] Ishtiaq Qureshi, *Ulema in Politics*, 231.

The post-1857 syndrome illustrated the unbridgeable gaps between the `ulama and the new opportunities to acquire modern education. The representatives of modernism in Egypt and India like Muhammad Abduh, Sayyid Ahmad Khan and Syed Ameer Ali saw no conflict between Islam and science. They harboured no illusions that the Islamic civilisation was the precursor to the European Renaissance and, therefore, possessed the innate potential to assimilate the scientific progress appropriated by the West. Of course, the Muslim modernists disregarded the negative impact of the rationalist trends which gave rise to Marxism and Communism and other hybrid movements, displacing religion in the collective life of man. Sadly, the Muslim countries were not immune to the pernicious influence of these isms.[37]

In its divide and rule policy, British colonialism, in particular, supported the deviant Islamic movements that served their political interests. Qadianism[38] rose from the ashes of obscurity in Punjab and worked in complicit with the British government to dislodge the concept of the finality of Prophethood (*khatm al-nabuwwat*). The `ulama's position was swift and decisive. Their writings and debates with the Qadiani cohorts stemmed the tide of the Muslim community falling prey to the conspiratorial campaign against the Holy Prophet (pbuh). Iqbal, the Poet of the East, made a profound remark regarding the Finality of Prophethood:[39]

Islam as a religion, consists of a uniform belief and the law, but as a social entity its existence rests on the creed of the finality of Prophethood. Islam can subsist on its law but the sense of Islamic unity springs from the belief in the finality of Muhammad's prophethood.

In an insightful article, Maroof Shah comments that Iqbal's interpretation is irrefutable proof that Islam as a *din* (way of life) has been perfected and there is no room for improvement, evolution or

---

[37] For a critical assessment of Marxism and Communism, see Ansari, *Islam versus Marxism* (Karachi, 1982) and *Islam and Communism* (Karachi, 1980). Cf. Khalifa Hakim, *Islam and Communism* (Lahore, 1994).

[38] Leading scholars undertook a critical study of Qadianism. See Elias Burney, *Qadiani Movement* (Durban, 1955); Abul Hasan Ali Nadwi, *Qadianism A Critical Study* (Lucknow, 1976).

[39] Muhammad Iqbal, *Harf i-Iqbal*, 136-7.

development.[40]

Tasawwuf in the Political Spectrum

Apart from the critique of these deviant sects, the modernists and the Salafi groups challenged sufism (*tasawwuf*) as the legitimate expression of Islamic spirituality. In the Indian context, *tasawwuf* had established itself as the transmitter of the universal values of Islam in a land dominated by Hinduism. The *mashā'ikh* were responsible for the mass conversion of Hindus to Islam through their distinct style of tabligh. Over the centuries, *tasawwuf* evolved within the Indo-Islamic cultural environment. As a result, the syncretic practices associated with popular Islam was evident. This did not imply that *tasawwuf* degenerated completely. On the other hand, the presence of the *mujaddids* (reformers) was responsible for realigning the course of *tasawwuf* to be shariah compliant.[41] Moreover, the amalgam of the sufi-'alim tradition provided a positive catalyst to establish the message of Islam in its pristine form.

Another development that took place was in the realms of political structures. Pan-Islamism which stood against the West's dominance of Muslim countries did in some measure allow for self-introspection of Muslim decline. Scholars like Mohamed Ali, Mawlānā Abul Kalam Azad played pioneering roles in the Islamic renaissance project. However, their focus was, by and large, on the liberation of India from the British rule.[42] Their contributions to the Islamic intellectual thought were interwoven with the nationalist aspirations composed of multi-faiths. The destiny of Islam, according to them, could be strengthened by pursuing policies that were best suited to the Indian cause. Their collective voice did not necessarily represent the unitary expression of Muslim aspirations. On the contrary, Mohamed Ali was committed to the corporate Muslim identity which outlined the blueprints of an

---

[40] Maroof Shah, "Legitimating the Modern Project" in *Hamdard Islamicus*: vol. xxxi, 13:20.

[41] A comprehensive account of *tajdid* in the subcontinent is given by Muhammad Mujeeb, *The Indian Muslims* (Lahore, 1986) 113-67.

[42] This vision is clearly evident in Mohamed Ali, *My Life A Fragment* (Lahore, 1966); Khaliq Ahmad Nizami, *Mawlānā Abul Kalam Azad and the Thirty Pages of India Wins Freedom* (Delhi, 1989).

independent Muslim country, Pakistan.[43] From the spectrum of Indian politics, Mawlānā Abul Kalam Azad and a number of ʿulama, by their unwavering standpoints, championed the cause of composite nationalism. In other words, Muslims could co-exist with the Hindu majority in the undivided India. It was the Partition of India in 1947 that determined the future of the Muslim collective identity. Mawlānā Siddiqui's efforts to advance the Pakistan cause among the Arab world were in many instances impressive.[44]

Tabligh: Multidimensional Approaches

There are several dimensions associated to Mawlānā Siddiqui's personality which are gleaned from his writings. Although they were limited owing to his preoccupation with tabligh and lecture tours, they, nevertheless, give an overview of the areas of his work.

Broadly speaking, Mawlānā Siddiqui presented a rational exposition of the Islamic faith and practice. For example, *The Universal Religion* and *Universal Teachings*[45] are relevant works as these discuss the phenomenon of religions and its relevance to mankind. The philosophical explanation combined with psychological observation is signposted in order to appreciate Islam as the universal religion.

Progressive orthodoxy, a term developed by his successor, Mawlānā Ansari was also indelibly etched in Mawlānā Siddiqui's writings about the Islamic faith and practice. A lucid presentation of the perennial sources of Islam are contained in *The Principles of Islam* and *The History of the Codification of Islamic Law*.[46] These monographs are an elaboration of the distinctive features of Islam. The codification of Islamic law as shown by the formation of the *madhabs* (schools of thought) - the formative years of Islam - reveals Mawlānā Siddiqui's

---

[43] Afzal Iqbal, *Life and Times of Mohamed Ali* (Lahore, 1979), 338-77.
[44] Qadri, *The Greatest Propagator of Islam*, 22.
[45] The monographs together with other booklets of Mawlānā Siddiqui have been compiled by Mawlānā Abdul Hadi al-Qadiri bearing the title *Dimensions of Islam*. Some of these titles were originally published by Makki Publications and Islamic Publications Bureau of Cape Town.
[46] Siddiqui, *The Principles of Islam*, (Karachi, 2002).

mastery over the Islamic textual sources. The last-mentioned monograph has a greater relevance today in view of the anti-*taqlid* movements that have attempted to undermine the *turāth* (legacy) as the integral component of the established schools of thought.

Mawlānā Siddiqui's spiritual credentials were reflected in the *tasawwuf* tradition. His stature as a Qadiri shaykh and his profound insight into the inner dimensions of Islam are derived from the influential works of the eminent *mashā'ikh* like Sayyid Abdul Qadir Jilani[47], Imam Ghazali, Rumi, etc. In a similar vein, *The Forgotten Path of Knowledge*[48] and the *Quest for True Happiness* are concise spiritual guidelines for the aspirants in the *tasawwuf* tradition. Mawlānā Siddiqui's scholarly presentation of *tasawwuf* is brought out in the *Spiritual Culture in Islam*. Like a spiritual physician, he diagnoses the maladies affecting the *ummah* and prescribes remedies that are life-enriching and meaningful. An important Urdu monograph, *Kitāb al-Tasawwuf*[49] belongs to the genre of classical sufi works. The eloquence, rhetorical powers and stylistic usage of language are compressed in this excellent work. In a specific sense, it is an accurate reproduction of the essence of *tasawwuf* explained by the *mashā'ikh* over the centuries.

The history of Islam had witnessed deviant sects making audacious claims to prophethood. The charisma associated to the founders of these sects was meant to distort the Islamic teachings by bolstering their false claims. Qadianism emerged during the period of political upheaval in India by coining new forms of prophethood. Mawlānā Siddiqui also contributed to the series of anti-Qadianism literature. His *A'ina Qādianiyat (The Mirror)* exposes the bizarre claims of Qadianism. Likewise, he edited a number of monographs to raise awareness in the Muslim world about this deviant movement.

Overall, the intellectual legacy of Mawlānā Siddiqui has been largely marginalised as no systematic study has been undertaken during the last seventy years. A number of his writings dealing with his intellectual contributions are no longer extant. Only *A Shavian and*

---

[47] Mawlānā Siddiqui's profound love for Shaykh Abdul Qadir Jilani is poignantly expressed in *Dhikr i-Habib* (Karachi, 2018).

[48] Siddiqui, *The Forgotten Path of Knowledge* (Karachi, 1980).

[49] Siddiqui, *Kitāb al-Tasawwuf* (Karachi, 1994).

a Theologian[50] offers a glimpse into his mastery of comparative religion, Qur'ānic studies and world history. This widely-acclaimed monograph had carved out a niche for Mawlānā Siddiqui as the erudite scholar of international acclaim.

Love for the Holy Prophet (pbuh) permeated the personality of Mawlānā Siddiqui. –Back to the Qur'ān' and 'Back to the Holy Prophet (pbuh)' bore the unmissable traces of his deep-seated attachment to the Holy Prophet (pbuh).

Belonging to this genre, *Dhikr i-Habib*[51] serves as a reminder to the *ummah* that love for the Holy Prophet (pbuh) and his *uswah al-hasanah* (excellent model) are true markers of the perfect faith (*imān*).

Western civilisation possessed the paraphernalias of superiority due to its imperialist policies. It also bought in its wake a number of Orientalist writings committed to undermining the Islamic civilisation and culture. 'The Backward nations of the East', a derogatory term applied to Muslims, was calculated to demean Muslims psychologically. One of the strategies employed by the Orientalists was to highlight Islam's unscientific worldview. Unlike the Muslim apologetics, Mawlānā Siddiqui wrote *Cultivation of Science by the Muslims*[52] to demonstrate Islam's enduring scientific outlook. Its legacy is concisely explained and supported by relevant Qur'ānic *āyāt* (verses).[53]

Democratic institutions with claims to the protection of human rights and equality had failed to counter the emergence of Marxism and Communism in the twentieth century. These **isms**[54] in turn were also existential threats to the Muslim countries, some of which embraced them after gaining independence from the colonial rule.

---

[50] Siddiqui, *A Shavian and a Theologian* (Durban, 1955).

[51] The Urdu books have seen several reprints in the subcontinent.

[52] Siddiqui, *Cultivation of Science by the Muslims* (Karachi, n.d.).

[53] Siddiqui, *How to Face Communism* (Karachi, 1955).

[54] This term (ism) has a long history of the anti-Islam rhetoric. In the twenty first century, it has assumed a rebranded form of hostility towards Islam. Islamophobia, is an instance in point. It is a global campaign by portraying Islam as anti-civilisation, anti-West, anti-human rights, etc. Indeed, it has deepened the Clash of Civilisations debate.

Egypt, in particular, promoted a rebranded version of Socialism to show that Islam was compatible with the wayward policies of this ideology. This growing menace prompted Mawlānā Siddiqui to write a critique of these movements. In his *How to Face Communism* Muslims were reminded of their obligations as *Khalifat Allah* (representative of Allah).

In the historical perspective, the world tabligh tours undertaken by Mawlānā Siddiqui did not offer him the opportunity to write comprehensive works on the myriad issues affecting the Muslim *ummah*. His series of lectures in countries were, however, recorded. Sadly, over a prolonged period of time many of his recorded lectures were lost. It was during his epoch-making lecture tours to South Africa in 1934 and 1952 respectively, that special arrangements were made to record and transcribe his lectures. *The Roving Ambassador of Peace*[55] is an edited version of the lectures delivered by Mawlānā Siddiqui in the Cape and other provinces.

In the following pages a thematic presentation of Mawlānā Siddiqui's varied contributions to the Islamic reawakening project is highlighted. Relevant passages from his writings and articles contained in the magazines and lectures (which have been transcribed) and arranged under specific topics provide an organic structure to his thoughts. This format is aimed at reinforcing the key themes that guided Mawlānā Siddiqui's tabligh mission. Also, the relevant historical information gives a clearer understanding of his writings.

A notable feature of the present volume is the inclusion of excerpts of articles, documents and historical photographs that have a direct bearing on his world tabligh tours. While a chronological narrative is not strictly followed, the resource material is a useful guide to assess his contributions to the countries he visited. Again, the political and historical settings as well as the social milieus under which he undertook these lecture tours, and on many occasions single-handedly, are examined to highlight his extraordinary achievements in response to the changing landscapes of tabligh.

---

[55] Yasien Mahomed, *The Roving Ambassador of Peace* (Cape Town, 2006).